Website Essentials

A Guide to Planning, Designing and Managing your Website

Philip N. Thompson

Frogeye Publications

First published in Great Britain in 2006 by
Frogeye Publications

Copyright © Philip N. Thompson 2006

Cover image and design by Red Arc Media

ISBN 10: 0-9553040-0-8
ISBN 13: 978-0-9553040-0-2

Printed and bound by Lightning Source Ltd

Acknowledgements

I would like to thank a number of people for their assistance and support. First of all, my family, Angela and Mat for putting up with my moods as I've locked myself away in my study typing for countless hours; the computing staff that I work with for the insight they have provided and the many students that I've taught for giving me endless hours of amusement and frustration but ultimately for testing out most of the technical issues I've discussed in this book.

I'd also like to thank my mum and dad for their time and investment that has provided me with the opportunities and education required to gain all the knowledge needed to place me in the position to write this book.

Finally I'd like to thank my closest friend Carol for all the inspiration and support offered in motivating me to finally complete this book and her partner Mark for the book's design.

So many elements have come together over many years: skills, the acquisition of knowledge, the meeting of people, the sharing of ideas and inspiration, the mention of a word or topic, and being in a certain place at a certain time. This has culminated in the end result - the production of this book. For all those unknown people that have influenced my path I'd like to thank all of them.

Disclaimer

Neither the author, nor the publisher shall have liability or responsibility to any person or entity for any loss or damage stemming from reliance on the information provided in this book.

Efforts have been made to verify the information given. However, there may be inaccuracies or misunderstandings. Therefore this book should be used only as a guide.

Contents

Introduction

Introduction

To be able to claim that you own a successful website involves taking a long journey through many processes. The aim of this book is to provide you with the essential knowledge and understanding of the principles needed for effective website planning, design and management.

In part one, you will learn how to plan your ideas and gain an understanding of the life cycle of a website and the stages that are involved in the development of a project. Having the foundations of your project in place will enable you to start the design process as described in part two.

Developing and designing the website is only part of the task. Part three discusses how you should manage your completed website regardless of its purpose. The principles covered can be applied to many types of websites and should provide you with the essential knowledge and understanding of how websites are managed in a commercial environment.

Part four discusses methods that you may consider incorporating into your website to help you earn some money in return for all the hard work you have put in developing your project. There have been numerous success stories from Google to the million dollar pixel advertising entrepreneur, but to construct a website that looks professional and makes money is a different issue. It takes a good idea, plenty of luck, sound business sense, creative skills in web page design, marketing and promotion and an ability to work hard.

So why have a web site at all?

Before the internet became readily available to everyone, businesses advertised in local newspapers, trade magazines and catalogues. They would become locally known through their customer base and by reputation. International businesses built upon their trade by using representatives that travelled from country to country advertising products.

Communication between the customer and the organisation existed only in the form of phone, fax or snail mail (postal service). While these types of service provided a satisfactory provision for business at that time, the introduction of the internet and email has increased opportunities for trade beyond comprehension.

Business with a client ten thousand miles away can now take place by email or by video conferencing. An email can reach its destination anywhere in the world in seconds, with a response returning equally as quickly. Video conferencing offers oral and visual communication with any one or even a number of people anywhere in the world.

Many new businesses have developed through the use of the internet which would have been completely impossible prior to its introduction. In the past, my own work as a freelance writer for publishers around the world would not have been possible without the internet. Email offers the opportunity to send articles to a publisher taking only seconds to deliver instead of days or even weeks. By having a good website a quality portfolio of work can be exhibited to potential clients. The services offered can be explained and contact details provided. By managing the site effectively money can be earned through advertising, affiliate links with other organisations and from the sale of products and services. No modern-day organisation should be without a website or email if it intends to survive or further develop in a competitive world.

Many of us have probably heard of a success story involving an individual that has made large amounts of money through a website. A simple concept can make millions if it is well thought through and implemented yet it never ceases to amaze me how fortunes can be lost by companies that do not manage their websites efficiently or effectively. If you are going to have a presence on the World Wide Web, then do it right and make a commitment.

The topic of Web Site Management not only applies to large international organisations, but SMES, (Small and Medium Enterprises) too. I have aimed this book at the everyday individual that wants to manage their own website for either personal usage or maybe for a business venture.

Based on my own skills and commercial experience, I hope that by the end of this book you will have gained an appreciation of the skills, knowledge and understanding required in producing what would be considered a successful website, and that you will have a go at applying those skills and knowledge for your own project.

Part 1
Planning
Your Website

1.1 Planning Preparation

The most important phase of web development is planning. Before you start choosing page layouts, writing content and preparing graphics, you must understand your website objectives, your intended audience and your site's architecture.

Websites can frustrate the visitor if they are not well-planned. Ultimately, you could lose the visitor's interest to the point that they won't return.

There are seven points to consider when planning your website:

- The purpose of your website.
- Your target audience.
- The technologies accessible to your target audience.
- How to go about attracting visitors.
- How to organise your information.
- The method of measuring whether you are successful.
- How you will manage your website project.

The purpose of your site

The design of your website should complement and enhance your site's purpose. Be careful not to overlook this essential rule.

Look at the following and see what category your proposed website fits in to:

- To sell a product or service.
- Persuade people to a particular action.
- Give information about an idea or issue.
- Increase awareness for your company.
- Improve the image of your company.

- Provide a service online instead of using traditional methods.
- Provide a service online to compliment an offline business.

If you have more than one purpose for your website, explore whether the purposes are compatible. If not, you could develop sub-sites within a larger website. For example, a computer company may maintain two sites: one for the general public and one for technicians where additional information and features would be available.

Throughout the creative design process and the preparation of content, you should consider every aspect against the site's original purpose. If the content or design doesn't further the purpose of your site, rework or remove it.

Your target audience

It would be nice to think that everybody on the web will visit your site, but that is unrealistic and unlikely. Your website will not appeal to everyone. When working on some of my web sites I have tested pages and design elements on a number of people. Some points have appealed to groups of people while other individuals have disliked a design element. I have come to the conclusion that you can't please all of the people all of the time. Focus on the target audience and what they will like and build your website to suit those people. Of course knowing what your target audience wants or will like helps. This could be a need for information, product or service or maybe a website that is easy to navigate. If you get it right, then you will have a responsive audience and find that you receive positive feedback through your questionnaires, feedback forms or through sales.

The first task is to ensure that your target audience has access to the internet and can use it. In one of my businesses, my target audience is the elderly. This is probably one part of the population that is not fully conversant with the use of the internet. However it is changing. More of the elderly are getting on the internet as each day passes. Analysis of my sales figures show that a large proportion of my website business comes from working individuals with a busy hectic life. Results also show the demographic area for my audience. You should carry out as much research as possible to discover where your target audience is and their behaviour patterns.

Check internet demographic information from Nielsen Net Ratings or from market research information available from your local library or trade associations. Find out about the background of your potential visitors and their potential requirements for your services. Discover what other sites they visit and find out about their internet usage. This information about your target audience can help you successfully design and market your website.

If you've already completed a business plan, this information will likely be part of the marketing section. If you don't have a business plan or a marketing plan for your business, this is the time to put one together. You can obtain advice from your local enterprise agency.

The key element of a successful marketing plan is to know your customers - their likes, dislikes and expectations. By identifying these factors, you can develop a marketing strategy that will allow you to arouse and fulfil their needs. Identify your customers by their age, sex, income/educational level and residence. At first, target only those customers who are more likely to purchase your product or service. As your customer base expands, you may need to consider modifying the marketing plan to include other customers.

Technology that is accessible to your target audience

Including the latest web technology on your web page isn't always the best idea. Not all visitors to your website can access this technology. There are many different browsers available and users are experimenting with alternatives to Internet Explorer and Navigator. Firefox is growing in popularity. Some of the browsers need additional plug-ins to be able to view the new technology incorporated in the latest websites.

It is also worth remembering that not everybody is willing or able to download the plug-ins. The company I work for part of the week has a policy that prohibits any downloads and has permission restrictions in place to prevent users accessing any part of the options or configurations menu of the browser. While I can visit most websites and make purchases, I can not visit those websites that require special plug-ins. If your target audience and their behaviour patterns show that they make purchases during the day due to their busy and hectic lives, then you are severely limiting or hampering the success of your website. So, make sure that the web technologies you plan to employ on your website are compatible with your audience.

Generally, it's best to design a site that is accessible to as many people as possible. If you are required to comply with the Disability Discrimination Act (DDA) regulations, you might also be required to provide an accessible website. This means limiting use of multimedia (audio or video), JavaScript, java applets, Flash, Shockwave, Adobe PDF, frames and dynamic html features.

If you choose to use web technologies that are not available to all your visitors, keep these guidelines in mind:

- Use features that are compatible with as many versions of web browsers as possible.
- Use features that degrade gracefully in browsers that can't display them so that the functionality of your website isn't affected.
- Provide alternative web pages for those visitors who can't enjoy leading-edge technology.
- Avoid creating a homepage that can only be seen with plug-in software.

Once your website is up and running, you can analyze your server log files to find out what types of browsers (and browser versions) your visitors are using. Then you can make better decisions about the types of technology to use. An essential pointer: Always test your website in multiple browsers to ensure the compatibility of your website.

Consider your website management plan

Creating a website can be enjoyable but consider who will have the final say over content and design. This is particularly important if you work in an organisation. Although you may have a web development team with everyone having a particular input, someone needs to manage the overall development and ensure that the site's goals are being met.

Plan in advance on how you will resolve problems. Decide who will make the final decision if any agreements cannot be reached. On the whole, it's better to organise this in the planning stages so that everyone concerned is aware of their roles in creating and managing the website's content.

Keep in mind that the largest expense of running a website is in the time it takes to manage it so if you work as part of a team, make sure it runs efficiently and without any conflicts.

Website Life Cycle

Understanding the life cycle of a website will provide you with the key processes you should follow to enable you to have the best possible chance of success.

A website usually follows a life cycle consisting of five stages:

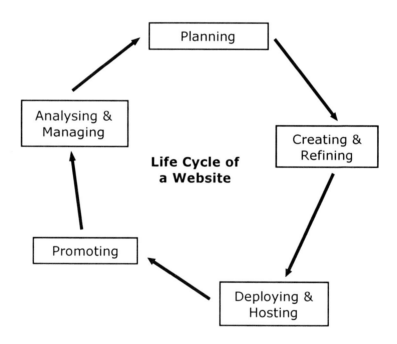

Missing a stage out is like trying to walk before learning to crawl, or maybe running before learning to stand on your feet.

I spend quite a lot of time during my working week teaching degree level students about successful website management. Every year a fresh intake of students appear; there are always a small group of students that decide that they know better and want to skip the planning stage and get stuck in to designing and coding their website. So, it's no surprise then when I also tell you that every year I see the same thing happen later in the Semester when problems start to develop through bad planning or, worse, no planning at all.

The life cycle may take anything from days to weeks to months to complete before coming full circle. The time element depends on the size of the project. I've also seen some projects that never get out of the planning stages, although these are usually projects run purely by academics with little experience of the real world.

If you can keep these five stages in mind at all times then you can't go wrong.

1.2 Planning Your Website

Many people attempt to sit down at a computer and start to create a website without thinking about the actual design. Having a clear understanding of the objectives of your website is crucial if you wish to be successful and stay within budget.

Consider some of the following guidelines to assist you in the planning stage:

- **Decide on a website objective.**

Decide on the purpose of the website. Think about the type of customer or client your website is aimed at and what you are going to offer your visitors. This will help in clarifying the steps you need to take.

- **Set a budget for the website project.**

Consider how many hours will be spent developing your website together with how much you can spend on advertising. You should also consider the number of hours that will be spent each month on updating your website. Not all jobs are paid by the hour. Content is usually charged by the word. Different types of content such as interviews with celebrities are charged at a higher rate.

- **Market Research.**

Look carefully at what the competition is doing. Check to see if there is a market for your product or service. See if there are any companies that can help you or offer services or products on your website. Carry out some research on market trends.

- **Structure your website.**

Sketch out the pages in storyboard format and include annotation with what you intend to place on the web pages. Look at how the pages should be linked together. Detail how you intend to place information and products for sale for the maximum impact.

- **Website content.**

Decide on what graphics and text you are going to include on your website. Consider what type of information you want your web pages to contain, and who will write the content. You should also consider whether you can guarantee the accuracy of the content if it contains technical details.

- **Decide on a theme for your website.**

Decide on a colour scheme and theme for your site. Consider whether there are any colours that relate or identify the product you are selling. Look at the company logo, graphics and text styles. Be consistent throughout to maintain your brand image so that your potential customers can clearly identify and remember you.

- **Affiliation with other companies.**

Set-up affiliation links with complementary websites. Look for companies that may want to advertise on your site, and decide on suitable locations where you intend to promote your own site.

- **A catchy domain name.**

Reflect on your domain name. This should be easy to remember and catchy. It may relate to a product or company name. Be careful not to use registered trade names or titles that may be copyright.

- **Hosting Options.**

Investigate the options for hosting your website. Research some companies that host websites. The location and country of your target audience may pre-determine the country in which you host your website. Consider the quality of service your hosting company offers, and the charges for hosting your website.

- **Features to include in your website.**

Adding a website search facility is an excellent tool for your visitors. It allows them to search large websites for information, services or snippets of articles that they are looking for.

It may not be possible to have a navigation button for every facility or item of information on your site. There are options. You can develop and code features yourself if you have a moderate amount of web design skill, or obtain some free code that will do the task for you. Many websites offer pieces of code that can be incorporated into your website.

1.3 Domain Names

What is a domain name?

It is a text name that is used around the internet community to represent the presence of a business or an individual. It is part of a system called Domain Name Service or DNS. This provides internet users with an easy to remember name that is converted into an Internet Protocol or IP address, based on numbers, such as 198.208.78.56.

Back in the early nineties when the internet was in its infancy, domain names didn't exist in the form we have them today. Internet users had to type in an IP address of a site to access and download information. Graphics were virtually none existent and the internet was just a text-based system.

A few websites still prefer to use the IP address instead of a domain name, however this makes finding the website almost impossible unless you know the IP address.

All domain names are prefixed by the protocol of http:// which means HyperText Transfer Protocol. This protocol identifies the website as a web page and not a FTP server. FTP (File Transfer Protocol) is prefixed by ftp:// and is usually home to news groups and downloads.

Do you need a domain name?

There are many free domain names available on the internet. The question I get asked most frequently by students is "Do I really need a domain name?" To answer this question you first need to consider a number of issues regarding your website project.

Owning your own domain name can offer many advantages over using one of the free domain names available. If you want to be taken seriously on the internet then it's a good idea to buy one, especially if you have a business. You don't want your competitor to grab your potential customers! The cost for a domain name is modest compared to the cost of maintaining your website. You can, however, use one of many free website services which offer free domain names or check what is available with your ISP (Internet Service Provider). This is great to get you started however it usually involves conditions such as allowing un-related pop-ups or a banner advertisement to appear on your website.

Picking a Suitable Domain Name

Your domain name represents your presence on the internet so consider your choices carefully. Here are some useful guidelines to follow:

- **Keep your domain name short.**
Users do not like to type in lengthy names and short names are more easily remembered.

- **Try a combination.**
Consider using a combination of letters and numbers. Try unconventional names, such as my2cars.com. Do bear in mind

though that they can create issues when it comes to searching for the name on the internet.

- **Make it 'catchy'.**

It should be easy to remember, so consider something catchy and appealing.

- **Advertise where your company is based.**

The letters used in the domain name that dictate the country of origin can help you in choosing a domain name. This will show people where your company is based. The main reason that .com is so popular is that it doesn't relate to any one particular country. However, if your market is focused towards a particular country, using the extension letters of that country could prove an advantage.

- **Think ahead.**

At some point in the future you may want to expand and have offices in other parts of the world. Check to see if your domain name is available in other countries. You may also wish to register and reserve these domain names for future use. There is no limit to how many domain names you purchase and register. However, mass registering of domain names or deliberately registering a domain name to prevent another individual or company use of that name is frowned upon.

- **Understanding the format of domain names.**

Up until November 1999 all domain names were restricted to a maximum of 23 characters in length plus the extension. Since the advent of new developments across the internet a number of registrars have started offering domain names up to 63 characters in length plus extension. To reiterate, short domain names are more memorable, however long domain names can be turned into a useful marketing tool. There are other restrictions to the choice of your domain name such as no spaces or punctuation marks, although a hyphen is acceptable. Some countries have a minimum length for a domain name that is usually three characters.

- **If your domain name has already been registered.**
Try different combinations. For example, if computersforyou.com has been taken, try computers-for-you.com or computers-4-u.com

You can also check companies that register or sell domain names and see if they have a list of domain names that are for sale. Most companies have a 'top ten' list of popular domain names that you can purchase, but for a price that is.

- **Using trade names.**
Avoid using other company brand names for your own website or business name. Some names are trademarked and unauthorized use could result in legal action.

Domain Extensions

What domain name options do you have available to you? The most popular choice is always a .com. However, as a consequence of being popular, most .com domain names have already been taken.

Other choices include using the letters of a country to enhance your domain name choice. This could greatly help in making your domain name a success. Sweden '.se', Portugal '.pt', and Iceland '.is' all provide useful extension letters that could be used with a suitably chosen domain name. It is ironic in that some third world countries have had their domain name extensions bought up by investors, who offer extensions like '.to', (Trinidad and Tobago), or '.md', (Madagascar).

If you are choosing a domain name for your company you may be considering a .com or a .co.uk. However if your company has an office in New Zealand you should consider checking to see if the same domain name with the .NZ extension is also available. Corporations like Microsoft like to keep the same domain name for all its world wide offices but just have the relevant country's extension change. So for my company I might have www.mycompany.co.uk and I would want to see if www.mycompany.fr is available for the French office and www.mycompany.de for the office in Germany.

Remember that different countries have different rules. In some countries, it's a 'first come first served' policy, whereas in other countries the rules are a little more complex and may require you to have an operational business based in that country.

During 2006 and 2007 a new range of domain name extensions will become available. This will further enhance the options available.

Choosing a reputable domain name company

Short-list a selection of reputable, well-known companies for your domain name purchase. Check out the domain name prices of these companies before purchasing as they can vary substantially. Look for a company that provides a physical address and is easy to contact by email or phone. Try phoning their support line and see how long they take to answer. Are they helpful? The time taken to respond to your email enquiry is usually a good indication of the quality of support. Read through any customer reviews that may be on the website or ask the company for some references directly from their customers. See how long the company has been established. Bogus companies don't tend to be in business for too long.

Costs involved

The cost of a domain name varies and depends on two things, namely what type of domain it is and which registrar you use. You can expect to pay between £10 and £35 a year for a .com/.net./.org and between £5 and £10 a year for a co.uk. As well as paying for the Naming Authority Fee you may need to pay a company to host the domain and point it to your site, but in most cases, this is included in the domain name purchase price. Check the small print!

Domain name availability

The opportunity to find the domain name of your choice is limited unless you have something unique and original. If your choice of domain name isn't freely available you might want to consider approaching the current owner and making an offer. Do realise that you aren't in the strongest position to dictate the price but it depends on your budget and how much you need this particular domain name.

Millions of names are mass registered by holding companies that then go on to sell the names at a higher price. It is not uncommon for some individuals to have made large sums of money through purchasing a simple domain name and selling it on. If you are lucky enough to own a domain name that is in demand by another individual or organisation, then you could be in line for a highly profitable take-over offer! I have experienced this from a company that once approached me to purchase my domain name www.better-it-skills.com for their own business.

Alternatively you should consider trying different variations of the name. Use hyphens or abbreviations for words: for example www.theplace2b.is . This is a clever use of numbers and letters to achieve a short but memorable domain name, married with an extension from Iceland. I've included a list of countries with their extensions in the appendix. If you spend a little time you can come up with some really catchy and effective domain names!

A problem with domain names like www.theplace2b.is that it is unlikely that users are going to find it by accident so you would have to focus on your marketing efforts so that visitors will find you.

To see if your domain name is available you should consult a Whois look-up tool. Whois is the database which records what domain names are taken and the contact information for them all. Many Whois tools exist on the internet and if you visit any website that sells domain names they usually have a look-up tool available to check domain name availability.

How do I register a domain name?

Once you have chosen a reputable domain name company and your domain name, you are ready to register your domain name. The task can be done completely online if you have a credit card, however make sure the company uses a secure server before providing your credit card details. Paying by credit card may offer you some protection too in case there are problems with the transaction. Check through the terms of purchase for any hidden charges before completing your registration.

What happens after registration?

As soon as you have chosen the domain name and made the necessary payment, it is transferred to a DNS Server where it will remain indefinitely as long as registration is kept up to date. You will then receive an invoice for the registration and some time later a certificate of registration for the domain name. Your domain name is held, usually for a one or two-year period, on the company's file server as well as with the domain name registrar such as Internic.

Now that you own the domain name you need to rent some web storage space and host your website. Remember you have only purchased the name, not the website or the space to host it. The next section will look at hosting in more detail. Once you have web space, you will then need to link your domain name to this space to complete the task. This is usually done through the online administration features that the company you registered your domain name with provides. If you have chosen a company that doesn't make a charge for this service then you can make changes as often as you want.

Since you can also have email addresses with your domain name it makes sense to choose something suitable. These emails are also forwarded through the company's file servers to your ISP mailbox. As it's a forwarding service, reliability depends on the quality of the company's file servers. If these fail, nobody can access your website. Some of the companies that register domain names charge for forwarding emails or for making changes to any details that they hold on their system so check the terms.

Domain Name Monitoring

Once you have registered your domain name, you might want to consider using one of the free Domain Name Monitoring services that are available. These services will send you monthly reports that make you aware of domain names registered by others that are similar to yours. With this kind of information, you will have the option to pursue legal action as a result of any trademark infringements or keep an eye on your competitors.

Owning a Domain Name versus Free Domain Name

If you are designing a personal website, using a free domain name is perfectly adequate for your needs. For a more professional outlook, it's recommended that you purchase your own domain name. Let's look at the advantages of owning your own domain name in comparison with using a free domain.

- **Your own domain name is easier to remember.**
To illustrate this, which is easier to remember? myhost.net/myownarea/longword/048739/yourname.html or yourname.com. You are much more likely to visit the second. Free domain names tend to be lengthy.

- **Your own domain name never changes.**
If you move your website to another server then the domain name does not change which means you never have to update links or submissions with search engines.

- **No advertising or pop-ups.**
Using one of the many free domain names available on the internet means that you are subject to the free host's terms and conditions. This may include having to endure advertisements in the form of pop-ups on your website. These advertisements or pop-ups may irritate your visitors.

- **Using email.**
When you have your own domain name you can have your own e-mail address (and sometimes unlimited ones) as well: yourname@yourname.com

URL Redirecting and Masking

Should you want to host your site with a different company, then the URL (Uniform Resource Locator) would change. So moving your website around or having multiple sites hosted would all cause problems with the URL.

One answer to the problem is to use one of the many web redirection services such as the one available from CJB.net. There are many others available so conduct a search in one of the web browsers for "redirection url".

Another answer is URL Masking or Cloaking. This facility is usually part of a package when purchasing a domain name. When a visitor types in your domain name and the browser finds your site, it is redirected to the site host and the URL of the host is usually displayed in the browser window. Masking or Cloaking the URL hides the host URL and maintains the domain name you purchased.

Some Useful Free Domains

Tokelau is a small place in Western Samoa. Fakaofo is the closest atoll to Apia. In September 2003, a delegation from the Dot TK team went to all three atolls to present what the Internet can mean for such a small country.

Foundation Tokelau, established in the Netherlands, financed the project. This Foundation has an advisory board with members of the community in Tokelau, and with members from the (anthropology) academic world.

Tokelau has now started offering .tk domain names for free. The island of just 1500 people have no real need for their own domain name extension even though they have been allocated one by ICANN.

The service is completely free as is the domain name, and with no advertising pop-ups. There is a drawback though: this is only a redirection service, not a DNS so you can not have a sub-domain name on it. Also you don't actually own the domain name. You do have full rights for its use though without restrictions.

If you want to obtain the license rights for your domain name, run your own Domain Name Server and also use your Dot TK domain for other services and hostnames, then there is a registration fee of $10.

Sub-domains

A sub-domain is also known as a "third-level" domain and is a way to create memorable web addresses for various areas of your site: for example http://mail.yoursite.com or http://help.yoursite.com.

Notice the three domain levels in the chart below:

http://	subdomain	.domain	.com
	3rd level	2nd level	1st level

There are many free sub-domain names available on the internet. A simple search in Google will reveal a list of companies.

The same problems exist with these free sub-domain names as with the free domain names. They usually all involve some advertisement being displayed on your website as part of the terms and conditions.

What is ICANN?

Internet Protocol (IP) addresses and country codes (ccTLD) Top-Level Domain names are managed and allocated by ICANN which is the Internet Corporation for Assigned Names and Numbers. This organisation is international and non-profit making. The task originally performed by a US government contract with the Internet Assigned Numbers Authority (IANA) is now performed by ICANN.

It is the responsibility of ICANN to ensure all the technical elements of the Domain Name Service works and that internet users can find valid addresses. All new TLDs (Top-Level Domain) names such as .com and .info and the new .eu are overseen by ICANN to ensure that they are universally accessible.

ICANN does not concern itself with legal issues regarding financial transactions or unsolicited email (spam), data protection issues. ICANNs mission is purely a technical one related to the DNS.

Looking Ahead for Domain Names

With the net registration market becoming more competitive, the kingdom of Tonga is actively marketing its ".to" domain name in the form of lifetime leases. To capitalize on the internet boom, the small island nation has teamed up with United States based company Tonic Domains. This will allow people to register ".to" domain names for up to 100 years for only

£1,500 or about £15 per year. Alternatively, Austria is offering domain names that end in ".at" which could be very useful.

The deregulation of the domain name business and the huge number of international domains has meant that it is very easy now to get a good domain name cheaply. During 2006 / 2007, a new range of domain name extensions will become available to further enhance the options. Move fast, however, as domain names are being registered at a rate of one every five seconds, according to networksolutions.com. Can you afford not to register your domain name?

Useful Resources:

Domain Names:
www.easily.co.uk
www.nominet.com

Free Domain Names:
www.20megsfree.com

Further Information:
www.icann.org

1.4 Hosting Your Website

Creating your website is only half the job; now comes the tricky task of where to host it. Do you host the site on your own computer on a dedicated server or with an ISP (Internet Service Provider)?

Hosting on your own computer or web server is more suitable for organisations with dedicated broadband lines and adequate resources to back-up the system. However, as broadband speeds increase and costs reduce, hosting your own web server is in the reach of everyone. I have hosted a web and FTP (File Transfer Protocol) server from home on broadband and appreciate the work involved in keeping it running efficiently and effectively.

Take the speed of dial up at 56Kbps and the speed you obtain when accessing a website and then divide by the number of visitors to the website. The more people that access your website the slower the speed of access will become. So you will need a wide bandwidth if your website is to work well. The type of website may also determine the bandwidth you require. If you are selling downloads like MP3s then a good bandwidth will be necessary. This may only be available through a dedicated ISP.

If you are hosting a small website for information purposes only then you may be able to do this through your 8mbyte broadband connection at home. I have successfully run a FTP server with a 2mbyte broadband connection, although the speed did drop when I got more than five users on at a time.

If you intend to host the website on your own server then you will need to install some web server software like IIS or Apache. Implement a firewall and possibly some user permissions. It would also be prudent to have your hard drive formatted with a NTFS (New Technology File System) partition to allow the required security measures to be put in place.

Alternatively I would suggest using an ISP to host your site. You can upload your website to one of their servers. The advantage to this is that the ISP supports the hardware side of things and this is the most popular hosting solution that people choose.

There are three main types of hosting available: dedicated, free or paid hosting.

Dedicated Hosting

Dedicated hosting is when your website is hosted by the company on their server with their connection. It is expensive and is only really a good idea for larger commercial websites.

Free Hosting

There are a great number of free hosting sites. One such site is Geocities. While the hosting is free, I always bear in mind that you only get what you pay for. Conditions may exist on free hosting sites that require advertisements or pop-ups to be displayed on your site when visitors are browsing your pages. Free hosting sites are generally slower due to the volume of traffic they receive and are quite often unsupported if you have any problems.

Most ISPs offer free web space when you purchase internet access through their monthly subscription. For example BTInternet.com offers a monthly internet subscription for broadband users, currently at £17.99 (prices are actually decreasing all of the time) which includes web space. However if you read the terms and conditions carefully you'll spot that BT like many other service providers prohibit the use of the web space for commercial use. If your website is personal and not for earning any great income then you'll probably get away with it. However if your website is selling a large number of products or services or likely to receive a heavy amount of traffic then it will probably ring alarm bells with the service provider. Most service providers offer commercial web space and the cost isn't that great.

Always read the Terms and Conditions. It has been known for free web hosts to claim the ownership of the copyright of your pages or not allow you to put your own advertising on the site! There may be special restrictions as to the type of content your website may contain and whether the site can be used for commercial purposes or not.

On the whole, free hosting is fine for personal projects but to get all the features and support that you will need for your commercial website, paid hosting is recommended. Of course, I am confident that after this book is published somebody will show me a free web hosting site that offers quality support, has a good set of features, no banner adverts and no pop-ups. But I stand by my remarks that you will get a better service if you pay.

Paid Hosting

If you pay for your hosting you are more likely to receive quality support and faster response times. In addition you'll get better features in your hosting package and since you are paying you'll be able to choose the required connection speed and bandwidth.

Paid hosting will usually cost between £5 and £75 per month. Dedicated servers will usually cost you over £150 per month.

Before committing to a paid web hosting service, ask them for a list of sites hosted by them. Visit some of the sites and test the speed of response. Email the webmasters and ask them how they find the service. What you are looking for is references. After all you are buying a service from the company that will affect your business and the potential income you will earn from it.

Before taking out any hosting package, I always email the technical support with a question and see how long it takes them to respond. If they can't reply quickly to a potential new customer then you have to ask what will their technical support be like when you have signed up for their service?

What hosting features do you need?

Now that you've short-listed some web hosting companies, what do you look for? Web hosts will offer you a range of services. Some of these may include:

- **URL/Address**: This is more important if you don't have your own domain name. Do you want http://www.ahost.com/alotoftext/bignumber/you/ or http://yourname.host.com (a sub-domain)?

- **Web Space**: The majority of websites take up only a small amount of space. A simple page with some graphics will probably only be 35KB. So 5Mbytes of web space will be quite adequate for the majority of websites. Graphics intensive websites or sites that have downloads might need more space, in the region of 15 or 20MB. Check out hosts that offer unlimited space although this is at a price.

- **Bandwidth/Transfer**: You should always ensure that you have adequate bandwidth unless you have a very small website. 1Gbyte/month should be the minimum. A hosting company will usually supply you with details of the monthly transfer allowable and the bandwidth available. Unlimited bandwidth is available but again at a price.

- **CGI-BIN** (Common Gateway Interface): Interactive scripts require the use of CGI-BIN. Counters, form-to-mail, and guestbooks are good features to include in your website. You can use free scripts but they will carry advertising for the site that provides them.

- **SSI** (Server Side Includes): This special function allows you to tell the server to include something on your page. It may be text or a CGI code. It's not usually required for small sites.

- **MySQL/PHP/ASP Support**: These are all database formats. Any inclusion of a database in your site and you will most likely need to use one of these formats. Nearly all sites use ASP (Active Server Pages).

- **Technical Support**: If you encounter any problems then you need to be assured that you can get help quickly by either email or phone.

- **Email**: Nearly all hosting companies will redirect email for you. Look for those that offer POP3 mail. This will allow you to connect directly to their system and download your messages. This feature is better than using a redirection service.

- **FrontPage Extensions**: Microsoft FrontPage is not a commonly used application within the industry. If you are using FrontPage for your site, then check that the extensions are supported.

- **SSL/Secure Server**: If you intend selling a product then you will need this to ensure your ordering process is safe.

- **Statistics/Log Files**: These files provide information about your visitors. They include files that have been downloaded and the pages that have been viewed.

- **FTP Accounts**: These are used for uploading files to your website space. If you have downloads available it is common to allow users to have anonymous access so they can download files.

Useful Resources:

NTFS:
www.ntfs.com

Free Web Space:
www.geocities.com
www.20megsfree.com

1.5 Your Website's Terms and Conditions

Over the years I have had experience of several websites and businesses and, from experience, have learned the importance of having adequate terms and conditions in place. I started my first website with only a few lines of terms and conditions and as different issues arose I added more. Today with my current business I have three full A4 pages of small print covering everything from war to acts of invasion! It sounds extreme but it's advisable to have all angles covered to protect your interests.

Having all these terms and conditions in place doesn't exclude you from your responsibilities as a web developer. You have to act responsibly to your web visitors. Look at the terms and conditions on other commercial websites for guidance and seek legal advice in drawing up the necessary documentation for your own website venture.

The Disclaimer

There are many issues that need to be considered as a legal adviser will tell you but the first one that I want to touch on is the disclaimer. The disclaimer is a way of bringing your visitors attention to the fact that you take no responsibility for any advice that you offer and that it is the responsibility of your customer or client to check out the validity of any such advice before acting upon it.

Be careful and aware of what you state as fact on your website, or in any advice or guidance that you offer. I once received an email from a student telling me he had tried something I described in one of my handouts on his computer and he had messed it up. I highlighted to him that my handout discussed the theory and what may be possible, but to be carried out only at the readers own risk. Make sure you include a disclaimer on your website so that your visitors are aware.

Copyright Laws

Copyright is a highly complex issue and you need to be aware of the legal implications and obligations where content is concerned. Many people are unaware that it is illegal to copy text or graphics straight from a webpage and use them in their own documents, websites or publications. Material such as graphics, text and even sound or moving image files belongs to the originator and is not necessarily free for you to use. You must obtain the originator's permission and maybe even pay a royalty for their use.

You can obtain royalty-free images and free copy on the internet if you search for them. Visiting the Press Office of companies will provide access to material and images that you can use.

From your own point of view, if you have produced an original piece of work, I suggest you place the copyright symbol © on your web pages where it can be seen to indicate that this work belongs to you or your company.

The internet has brought about access to an astonishing amount of information. It is quite likely that with sufficient searching you will find similar articles and pieces of information but great care must be taken that you don't copy or use copyright protected material. A breech of copyright laws can result in costly legal action.

Your Mission Statement

Many companies now have a mission statement for their business and on their website informing customers of the organisation's aim and purpose, and the level of service the customer can hope to achieve. These mission statements mean very little if the organisation and everyone working within the company do not buy into the whole ethos of the mission statement. By all means put your mission statement on your website, but make sure you live up to it.

1.6 Website Heuristics

Heuristics refers to the guidelines that you should follow for the design of interfaces. It is a process which uses the most appropriate problem-solving technique from a range of methods to ensure the successful next step is implemented in your web design. In the industry, it works on what we call 'rules of thumb'.

Some design issues to consider include:

- Having an online text file such as a word document or pdf file for the user to read. It interrupts flow and the user may not be able to print the whole document.

- Using CSS (Cascading Style Sheets) can help in your website design but can also disable your browsers ability to resize text.

- Having solid blocks of text intimidates the user. Break it down with bullet points, sub headings and short paragraphs.

- Be careful with your advertising. Bombarding your visitors with unexpected adverts is not advisable. The skill is in making your adverts not look like adverts and so avoid "banner blindness", "animation avoidance" and "pop-up purges".

- Don't open up new windows on your website to display pages. It disables the user's ability to use the back button.

- Don't ignore your users' needs. They visit your website because they want something. Failing to list a product price or pertinent information are good examples of what not to do.

- Avoid garish colours and colours that do not complement like red on blue or a green background.

- Don't place a counter on your site unless it serves a purpose other than to say you've only had two visitors today.

Some good points to ensure your website is more successful are:

- Ensure your visited links change colour.

- Make sure you have completed your Meta Tags. They can form a valued tool to encourage visitors to your site as the title forms part of the indexing process within a search engine.

- Consistency is one of the most powerful usability principles. Buttons should always behave in the same way throughout your site. Make your users feel in control.

- Always keep your users informed, such as on the progress of a download or whether a feedback form has been accepted or acknowledged.

- Use a language appropriate to the website users.

- Be prepared for users to make mistakes; give them the opportunity to correct them.

- Error prevention is better than attempting to correct the errors once they enter the system. An undo button gives users the opportunity to correct a mistake.

- Minimise the load on the users' memory. A user doesn't want to access a page via a long path.

- Flexibility and efficiency help the user by speeding things up. Keep this in mind for the completion of online forms, etc.

- Keep dialogue boxes simple and don't use any unnecessary wording.

- Provide a help facility. Give explanations of any potential error messages and what action the user should take.

- Make sure all graphics load quickly. Users get bored and won't wait long for pages to load.

- Keep the page design simple. Avoid overcrowding the page.

Storyboards

The first part of any design is to consider the desired look of your website. How do you want your pages to appear? I spend considerable time browsing through websites and taking screen captures of web pages and then writing brief notes on the printouts of my likes and dislikes about the design.

Too many people sit at their computer and start to code or construct their web pages without the necessary design considerations. I am a firm believer in planning and this stage involves the production of `storyboards'.

A storyboard is like a set of architects' plans for building a house. They detail the layout and structure of all the key elements. This enables the builder to construct the product with minimum guess work.

Storyboards can take any form you like although I usually draw out a box to represent the screen and write or type in where my content or text is going, the navigation buttons, colour themes and graphics. Annotate your storyboards; the more information, the better.

You may need to do several drafts of storyboards before you reach a final set of satisfactory designs. These can be presented to a client, customer or your team for approval before work starts on the coding of the website.

Part 2
Designing
Your Website

2.1 Website Design Principals

Having a website is becoming a necessity in the commercial world. It enables businesses and organisations to reach their customers and clients with minimal cost and maximum effectiveness.

Whether your website is for information purposes only, selling a product or service, or for gathering information, it will most likely have been designed with Flash, JavaScript, or just plain HTML. The following is a list of guidelines that you should take note of when designing your site.

- **A website that is easy to locate on the Internet.**
To reiterate, a catchy but simple domain name helps. It makes the website easy to find.

- **It makes good business sense to have your website available 24 hours of the day, 7 days of the week.**
Choosing a quality ISP and hosting company is critical to ensure continuity of service.

- **Visitors get bored if your index page does not load within 20 seconds.**
Graphic files can slow the speed that a web page loads, so bear in mind when you're placing images in a page, that each graphic file is no larger than 36Kbytes.

- **A web page and website should be easy to navigate; users like to be able to find their way around a website.**
A thought-out and structured website has good navigation routes. Ensure hyperlinks and buttons are clearly marked and are not ambiguous.

- **All content on a website should be updated on a regular basis.**
Check the content of your website for items of information that may be out-of- date, such as attractions, events or sales that have expired. Out-of-date news and content should be removed.

- **Ensure that your website has information that visitors need.**
If the content on a website is not useful then the visitors will not return. Make sure all content is accurate, up-to-date, useful and helpful.

- **Balance graphics and text on the web pages to appeal to users.**
A good structure and layout is critical to make a website appealing to visitors. Too many graphics and not enough text are as bad as too much text and not enough graphics. Keep the size of the graphics in proportion with the page size. Text should accompany each graphic as an explanation. Graphics help to explain the meaning of the content.

- **Consider the issue of security.**
Users don't like their details spread around the internet. A terms and conditions statement on your website explains how their details are used. Whether you intend to sell or share visitor details amongst other companies or if you intend to use the information for marketing purpose you should inform your customers.

The World Wide Web is constantly evolving and staying ahead of your competition is a challenge. Adhering to the above guidelines will help in designing a quality website and in offering a quality service.

The Logic of Web Page Design

There is one factor to web design which, if followed correctly, can help you develop a more successful design. This doesn't need graphical expertise, programming knowledge or business skills. It revolves around logic and common sense.

Getting the structure of your web page right is important to making your site successful. There are many view points of how a page is viewed by users, especially on issues like eye movement. The first place a user looks is usually at the top of a page and towards the left hand corner. This is exactly the reason why the majority of websites place their logo at the top of the page, as it instantly allows the user to identify the website that they are visiting.

The positioning of other elements on the page is also of great importance in making a design functional. It is logical that the main navigational links be placed in a bar on the left or along the top of a page. This is traditional with how we read a book in the Western world. We read from left to right and top to bottom.

In other languages where sentences are read from right to left, and sometimes bottom to top you may find the page design varies. If you view a website developed for this target audience you may find the navigation on the right. Although this is logical for this website's main audience, you will probably find it confusing. This is why, if you are developing for a predominantly Western audience, you should do the logical thing and place the navigation on the left or at the top, even if you want to have a strange new design on your site.

It is also logical that once you have finished reading a page whether in a book or magazine, that you turn the page rather than returning to the beginning of the book. You should also apply this principle to web design. When you finish reading a page on a website, you don't want to keep returning to the home page before going to the next page. To avoid this kind of problem you should consider providing a second type of navigation such as a set of icons or a simple set of links at the bottom of each page. This kind of backup will make your site easier to use.

Another page design consideration is whether you are unduly distracting your visitors. Personal home pages are renowned for using flashing animations and sometimes sound or media clips. Unless they play an active part in the main content of the page they should be removed. This is because they are highly distracting (which is why many adverts are animated or flash). Your users have come to the site to view the content, and you should do your best to please them.

2.2 Structuring your Web Pages

Another consideration of website development is the overall structure of the site. Three basic structures exist: hierarchical, flat and walkthrough. It takes a little logic to decide which one is best for you.

Some sites, such as Yahoo and Land Rover Discussion forums, use a hierarchical structure, where pages are in sections and sub-sections. This is a good method to store a large amount of categorized content. Navigation for all levels of the design should be provided, although navigation options from other categories can be hidden. Keep the clutter to a minimum.

The walkthrough style is less popular, where the user starts at one page and follows through the pages on a set path. This is difficult to achieve successfully, but works well for online ordering and tutorials.

Flat sites are not particularly common. The best example is probably a basic news site, where the latest stories are linked from the main page. This is simple to implement, but if you are following this route it can be tricky to keep the site easy to use, as there are often many options presented to the user.

You should probably have an idea what category your site fits into, and by applying this logic you can create a structure for the site.

Navigation Hints: Let the User Know Where They Are

Effective navigation is often overlooked by many webmasters, and it is a major mistake. The common assumption is that users will enter your website by the index page and go from there to the information they want by use of the navigation links. Unfortunately, this isn't always the case. A large number of your visitors will probably arrive at your site through search engine indexes that have listed a specific page within your site. If this happens, the user may have no idea where they are on your site. This is easy to overcome.

One method of letting users know where they are on your site is to use meaningful URLs. This works especially well with a hierarchical structure. For example, at Better-IT-Skills, many people enter the site via the portfolio page. If you look at the URL - better-it-skills/portfolio.htm it is obvious that this page is about a portfolio. It also helps, as the user can then delete part of the URL and return to the site's main page.

You can take things a little further by the use of a 'breadcrumb trail'. A breadcrumb trail is often found at the top of many sites. It is basically a textual representation of the site or directory structure, showing where the user currently is. Basically it's a mini site map in text form. Each item in this structure or site map is linked, so the user can easily access different pages. A breadcrumb trail is a very useful method of improving usability and is easy to implement.

Another method exists to let users know where they are on your site. This method works best with the 'walkthrough' type of structure. If you are on a site like Amazon ordering a product, it is often helpful to be told the current stage of your order. This usually takes the form of, for example 'Step 1 of 6' but an even better way is to use a graphical representation of all the stages in the process, and just highlight the current one. This will make your visitors much happier.

These methods of improving your site and design are actually simple and present some of the best ways to improve your site, making visitors happier and increasing 'stickiness' and sales.

2.3 Creating and Refining your Website

Once the specifications have been decided and the budget agreed, the design stage can commence. Consider the following points:

- **Develop a well structured Site.**
Ensure that you allocate logical file names to the web pages you have designed. This also goes for any graphic files included on your website. A suitable folder or directory structure is also critical.

- **Design a well thought out User Interface and Page Layout.**

Ensuring that users can navigate a website with ease is important. Once a theme has been decided upon, choose graphics and images that follow the theme. Acquire content that can be easily updated and is relevant to the site theme. Decide upon a resolution and colour range that suits the majority of your visitors.

- **Make use of any existing Content.**

Attempt to make use of any existing content, graphics or images available from your organisation, such as logos from business note paper or calling cards, even images and product descriptions from company brochures. Adapting this information for use on your website can save costs and time. If you are using a CMS (Content Management System) then integrate the content into your layout/format.

- **Develop New Content.**

Create additional content to supplement existing material and to keep the pages up-to-date. Apart from text, consider graphics, illustrations, photographs and animations.

- **Develop Perl, VBScript, CGI, or JavaScript Code.**

Adding Flash text or buttons, roll-over effects, or calculations most often requires some kind of script code to be added to your web page. Not all web browsers may have a plug-in that will allow these scripts to run. Keep this in mind when building your website and if you insist in using the script then maybe offer a link for visitors to download and install the plug-in. You can sometimes test to see if the plug-in is already installed and possibly offer the user an alternative page without effects.

- **Set-up Links.**
Look at cross-links within your site, such as a text link to another section. Links to related sites and links to advertisers all add value to your site when being listed by search engines.

- **Optimize Graphics.**
All graphic elements should be optimized to speed up download and avoid non standard colours. Each graphic should not exceed 36Kbytes. If you have a need to include a quality image on your website then use a thumbnail image on the page linked to a higher quality downloadable one. This will save time loading the page. Another trick is to fragment an image on a web page. Breaking a picture up into smaller cells allows each cell to load part of the image simultaneously speeding up the overall loading of the picture.

- **Proof Reading.**
Having spelling mistakes on a web page really does make the site look unprofessional. Rest assured if somebody spots a mistake on your web page, they'll take pleasure in pointing it out to you. I've been there before. So, ensure you don't have any spelling or grammar mistakes on your web pages. A professional image is essential.

Additional Design Considerations

Being found by the search engines begins with building a site that can be easily indexed and categorized. While there are hundreds of search engines on the internet, 90 percent of the traffic goes to the better known such as Google, Yahoo, AltaVista, Lycos and Excite. The method that each search engine uses to index web sites differs, so it is important to use all the tools available:

- Use descriptive **page titles**. These titles are coded into your web pages and appear in the title bar of browsers.

- Use well-worded **meta tags** (description and keywords). Meta tags allow you to specify keywords and descriptions for your pages. These are the same keywords that people enter when they are searching for products, so carefully consider what words your prospective audience might use to find you.

- Create **well-written content**. Use keywords in your content and avoid having a graphic-only front page.

- Try to **avoid frames** and dynamically-generated pages unless it is essential. Avoid Flash pages. Some search engines can't index framed or dynamically-generated pages, so avoid these technologies for your home page.

2.4 Navigation and Interface Design

In one of my classes, I teach HCI (Human Computer Interface) design. I've never found a student that enjoyed the subject, yet it is one of the most important topics that help in web page and website design.

A website without clear navigation is a website doomed to fail. An important heuristic is good navigation, and easily marked exit points. A clearly marked button saying `HOME' is evidence of this, and always points the users back to the main page. Relying on the browser navigation buttons is a bad idea; not everybody likes to use them. Have a look around the internet at popular websites and see where they have placed their navigation bars. Make sure all your navigational links are easy to find. Any links within content are usually marked as blue and underlined indicating it as a hyperlink.

I actively encourage all my students to use tables within web pages. All content, buttons and graphics should be placed within a table and locked down to a specific pixel size to prevent resizing when being viewed through different browsers or varying resolutions. Navigation buttons should be placed within cells within a table.

Alternatively you may wish to use a frame and place your navigational buttons with an HTML page in a frame. Frames were very popular several years ago but some web designers now shy away from them because of their lack of popularity with search engines. The concept behind the use of frames is that the window you view the web page in has been split into two or more separate pages. Each frame contains a separate web page. This technique enables the web designer to place the content of the web page in one frame and the navigation in another. The benefit of using frames is that to update the navigation only requires minimal changes, usually just one HTML page.

Unfortunately the disadvantage to using frames is that as previously mentioned, search engines are notoriously bad at indexing them. This is because they may index a page without navigation or just a navigation page without content. My personal opinion is only use frames for non-commercial sites or where necessary.

My suggestion is that if the website is intended to consist of only a few pages and not grow into a large site then go with a table. Should you need to update the navigation buttons it won't be a massive exercise to go through the pages and make alterations. If you are using frames then I would suggest offering a no-frames version of your website for those people that have trouble viewing frames within their browser or for the number of search engines that will not index websites with frames. If you use tables there is no need to worry about the search engines indexing your site or having to offer a different version. There are a number of tutorials on the web discussing the issue of Frames versus Tables.

Updating Your Website's Navigation

Apart from adding content to your website, replying to those endless emails and then checking through the website for out-of-date information, the next most time consuming task is making small changes to the navigation on your site.

Most sites start off small and grow. This is particularly true of information-based websites. Through lack of planning, a website that rapidly expands to hundreds of pages can result in disarray if content isn't properly managed. There are several solutions to this problem that can help to ease the task.

Using the Search and Replace function within your web page development application is one of the simplest and easiest methods. This involves entering the text or link that you want to search for and then entering the new link or code you want to replace it with. Each time you make a replacement all you have to do is click on the "Find next" tab in the search and replace box and proceed through the pages. Depending on how many pages you have and how you have structured your website will determine the ease of this task and whether you accidentally miss any links or replacements.

There are programs available on the internet that will do this task for you. However the technique as a whole does have a disadvantage in that a small mistake in the search or replace text will result in your design not working correctly. You also will need to upload your pages again to the host.

2.5 What is SSI?

Server Side Includes (SSI) is a system used on some servers that allows you to include files into your code when executed on the web server. This would mean that you could, for example, include navigation as a text file on the server, then place a special pointer to that file which then tells the server to include the contents of the text file, such as:

```
<!--#include virtual="/myfile.txt" -->
```

This can be very beneficial as it allows the storage of the navigation as a single file, like frames, so you only need to update one file to change the whole navigation of the site. Because it is server generated, there are no concerns about problems arising with search engines or browsers being compatible.

A disadvantage with this system is that the server must be able to support SSI for it to work. You should check with your hosting company to see if this is available.

Other Scripting

There are a number of other methods that you can use to achieve a similar effect as using SSI. One of these is PHP (Hypertext Pre-processor) and ASP (Active Server Pages). If you decide to redevelop your website at some point, then creating a database controlled website would be a good idea. This would allow you to control everything, including the navigation, meaning less work on updating the navigation at a later date.

Updating your navigation or other design elements needn't be a chore. With a little bit of forward planning and some skilled use of software, you can easily and quickly make updates, leaving you more time to do the important work.

Useful Resources:

PHP information:
www.php.net

2.6 Content Provision

No matter how well your website is designed its success will be severely hampered if it doesn't contain quality content.

So what is content? Content generally refers to the written or pictorial material or information found on the website. Good quality content can mean the difference between your visitors returning to your website or just visiting once. Quality content can also mean getting listed by major search engines or within professional publications or directories.

One of my first websites lacked sufficient content to keep visitors coming back. This was mainly due to my lack of experience at the time; I was younger then and less knowledgeable. I discovered the cause of the problem through analysing the web traffic and from a rather pointed comment made by my father. He politely informed me that he enjoyed visiting my site each day for the news link that I had scrolling across the index page. This news link was a real-time link to CNN and scrolled the day's news headlines across the webpage. It was at that point I realised that although I had made a good decision to include the news window, I had under-estimated the power of quality content on the website to keep visitors interested.

Of course apart from the inclusion of quality content, it is nothing if not kept up-to-date. How many times have you visited a website that advertises an event that was a year ago and no longer valid? As a visitor or customer I wonder about the commitment the company or individual has if the task of updating content is too much for them.

Increasingly search engines are ignoring the traditional method of reading the meta-tags for keywords and descriptions, as these are often abused by users. Instead, search engines like Google now read the whole web page and use it to generate matches. It stands to reason that the more pages and words you have the more probable your site will be returned as a search result.

A slightly sneaky trick to employ on your website is to use 'White Text'. Of course this has to be on a white background to work hence the title. I suppose you could have black text on a black background but I guess you get what I mean. The idea behind it is to fill spaces on your web pages with white text on a white background. Obviously this text is invisible to the user but will be picked up by the search engine and used to index the page within its database, based on the `invisible' content.

Having good quality content on your website will also assist in developing links with other websites and help to bring in more visitors to your site. The more links you have on your site the better the rating with search engines.

The main reason for having good content is that it will make your website popular with your visitors and has the best chance of surviving and doing well.

Now that we've established that good content is essential, let's consider how we go about getting suitable material.

Generating Your Own Content

By far the cheapest way to generate content is to write it yourself. However this may not be the easiest way to do it. Writing quality content takes time, good writing skills and knowledge of your subject. If you have the skills and time to generate content, this is the best route to take. You will be guaranteed to have exclusive content and will own the copyright.

Like many people I usually struggle with motivation and focus when it comes to working on large projects, so try to set a schedule with regular deadlines for completion of small pieces of content. This will allow you to stay motivated and see that progress is being made towards the overall project.

Content Providers

Another way of generating content is to get other people to write it for you. This method is often employed by commercial and corporate websites. Many organisations will have a team of content providers or selected key individuals that can provide small pieces of content that contribute towards the overall content management system.

If you are contracting writers to produce content for you then the cost can be anything from 20p per word upwards to £1 per word. Choosing the right people for the job is critical. If cost isn't an issue and you want a large amount of quality content written then this is the way forward.

Visitor Generated Content

I recently helped to develop a web project for a woodlands trust. It was a content management system. The web project itself was just an infrastructure to hold content contributions from visitors. Once the website was hosted, visitors would log on to the site and contribute articles, photos, and event information. All this content was then stored in a database and redisplayed on various pages within the website.

Getting your visitors to contribute the content is another method. Constructing a suitable content submission form for inclusion on your website helps to structure the layout of the content being submitted. Using a discussion forum or news room to contribute content is also a method worth considering. They are both cheap and easy to do. However you will need all the visitors you can get to make it work.

Syndicated Content

Going back to the first website I created and the news feed I included, this method of content provision is called syndication. Many organisations provide free news feeds or video feeds that can be included on your website. Because the feed includes a headline or logo to their own site, they are quite willing to give you the feed for free. Conditions are usually attached and quite often state that you should place a by-line at the bottom of the page, or a logo where visitors can see it.

Whichever way you choose to generate your content you must remember that it is the most vital part of your website.

However good your design or however fast your site, people come for content and that is what you should be giving them.

Add a RSS feed. RSS (Real Simple Syndication) allows content providers to syndicate their material and is quite popular where news feeds are concerned. You can use RSS feeds to gain free content from other sources to enrich your site or you can syndicate your own material.

You should consider 'real world' situations when attempting to understand syndication. An artist drawing a daily cartoon may make the drawing available to any newspaper that wishes to print it, in exchange for a fee.

Syndication of web content via RSS is not likely to make you very wealthy. But, it can be a good method of attracting attention to your site and attracting visitors. I have used an RSS feed on one or two of my own sites to attract traffic and keep visitors returning.

Website Stickiness

Stickiness is one of the most overlooked aspects of website promotion. Webmasters go to great lengths to optimise their sites for the search engines, and find the right keywords to place in their site's meta-tags, but this is all wasted effort if your site isn't `sticky' enough to retain your visitors.

If your visitors spend less than 30 seconds on your website it is more than likely that your site is not sticky.

There are many ways to make your site sticky, the simplest being to remind your visitors to bookmark your site. Create a bookmark button on each web page to make the task even easier for the user.

Ask your visitors to subscribe to a free newsletter for updates. This will enable you to capture personal information about your visitor and target them when you update certain pages that may be of interest to them. You may want to offer the visitor a free gift or access to downloads, something they find hard to refuse but need to register to obtain.

Having quality content makes your web pages interesting. It is the reason we go back to a site. Consider your own experience when visiting websites. What factors make you return to one particular website again and again? Is it for the content, news, forums, freebies or special offers? Making your site sticky will make all the difference when it comes to running a successful website.

2.7 CMS - Content Management Systems

A content management system is an application that has been specifically designed to manage a website. It can be integrated into a website to deliver content from a database to be displayed within a web page.

The principle behind a CMS is that it provides an easy method of updating content within the technical requirements of the web developer to post up new content. Adding new pages, deleting or editing all takes place within a database and then the web pages pull the information from the tables and display it. Menial tasks are automated such as applying page layouts and being consistent with the layout across the web site. Any website that consists of more than six pages and involves content on the pages that requires regular updating would benefit from a CMS.

After investing money in the development of your website each alteration or update involves further expense. Updating the content every month could be a costly task, but with a content management system this removes the expense and the requirement for technical expertise.

There are benefits to using a CMS as follows:

- You are no longer dependant on web designers to make amendments to the content of the website.

- Changes can be made at any time or as frequently as required. This allows your business to keep up-to-date.

- Less technical skill is required by content providers as the CMS handles layout and format.

- More than one person can make contributions to the site through the CMS.

- Consistency through all the pages is maintained.

A small CMS is not that expensive to construct and is not beyond the skill level of the intermediate web designer. Experience in database construction is required and an ability to link the database to the web pages.

Most organisations seem to recognise the need for a CMS. It will help you achieve your goals more easily, creating flexibility within the website and allowing you to stay ahead of your competition. With the growth of Ecommerce a CMS will support sales by providing product information and will complement the ecommerce infrastructure.

For a business to grow and expand it has to be able to change and adapt quickly. A CMS should provide the following:

- Improved business responsiveness.
- Improved publishing process.
- Reduced legal exposure.
- Supported website growth.
- Streamlined information updates.
- Improved knowledge sharing.
- Improved staff efficiency.
- Reduced customer support costs.
- Reduced publishing costs.
- Reduced website maintenance costs.
- Increased website audience.

Once you have defined the goals for the CMS, you can begin the requirements process. You should map each requirement to a specific business goal. The requirements specify the 'what', while the goals are the 'why'.

For example a business goal of `reduce website maintenance costs', may lead to the following requirements:

- Streamline the content provision process.
- Evaluate the CMS and the processes that are in place.

A content management system's life cycle is not too dissimilar to a website life cycle.

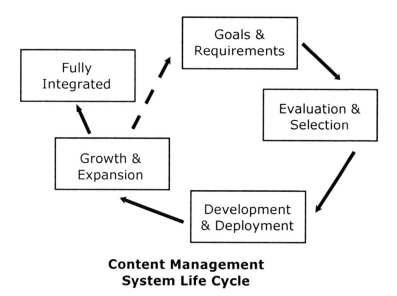

**Content Management
System Life Cycle**

A successful CMS depends not only on the technology but software and people. Selecting and implementing the right system are difficult tasks and there are issues that have to be addressed. It requires team involvement including authors creating content, editors, proof readers and then end users checking and reading through the content.

Do you need a CMS?

My current college teaching role involves preparing notes for students. The college I work in has a CMS for teaching staff to place their notes online for student access. Some staff use it, others don't. I am one of those that don't. So what are the issues that result in my failure to use the technology? In this particular instance, the answer is that there are easier alternatives available than the CMS.

Keep in mind:

- CMS does not always meet the needs of the user.

- CMS is not easily accessible to the end user or the authors.

- Time available to format the content because of lack of features available within the CMS can be an issue.

- Use of CMS does not always enhance the end product.

A successful deployment requires the active involvement of many staff. Many content management systems have been deployed in organisations with brief configuration, a rapid roll-out and a lack of consultation with authors or stakeholders. These are all necessary for a CMS to be successful.

While a CMS may be implemented, the lack of real cultural change means that a critical mass of usage is not obtained, and so the long term viability of the CMS is far from certain.

For a CMS to grow and expand it has to be adopted by the staff and meet the business goals. If this does not happen then the system will fail. Without growth and expansion the system can not become fully integrated and so the life cycle ends.

Authoring for a CMS

If you are part of a larger organisation, do you choose centralised or decentralised authoring for a CMS? Whichever method that is selected, the aim is to obtain quality content that is technically accurate and can be updated frequently. Both scenarios have their pitfalls, and in some cases a mixture of both can be the answer.

Centralised authoring involves a dedicated team responsible for creating the content for the CMS. They will create, manage, edit and publish the content. The team may consist of technical writers, editors, journalists, or subject matter experts. A close working relationship between the team members ensures there is quality content provision.

Some of the advantages of having centralised authoring are:

- Professional team members to ensure quality of content.
- Centralised location for feedback.
- Support.
- Reduced costs.
- Proactive and driven task force.

Some of the disadvantages of having centralised authoring are:

- Reliance on dedicated staff and resources.
- Potential content congestion.
- Requires improved communications for updates to take place.

Communications between the team and the rest of the organisation are essential to meet the business needs.

Decentralised authoring is usually adopted in most organisations as it is considered more cost-effective. In this scenario the authors are scattered amongst the remaining employees and departments.

Advantages of a decentralised authoring system are:

- Many authors can contribute to the system.

- Potentially more cost-effective.
- Reduces the need for a large dedicated team.
- May provide more up-to-date content.

However there are also disadvantages:

- Pre-existing workloads can hamper authoring.
- Motivation and resistance from staff can delay updates and deadlines.
- Authors have to be trained on how to use the CMS.
- Configuration of workstations to enable access.
- Higher costs in licensing software.

I have found that although a decentralised model is often adopted by organisations, unless the authors are fully supported by the organisation then the disadvantages out-weigh the advantages.

Useful Resources:

Mambo CMS is a popular and successful open source content management system that is used widely. It gives the user and multiple-users full control of content management and is particularly favoured by busy web designers who prefer to give CMS control to their clients. For more information, visit www.mambocms.org

2.8 Organising Information

How to categorise the information on your website is often the most difficult decision. If you are selling products, then getting the right categories and subcategories is essential to ensure customers quickly find the product they want. Although visitors won't move through your website from beginning to end like a book, the book metaphor is helpful in thinking about site organisation. There should be a table of contents, similar information should be grouped together, information should flow from simple to complex, and related topics should be cross-referenced.

Think about the information you want to offer and what you know about your audience, then try to determine if you should build a wide, shallow site (with many categories, but less content in each category) or a narrow, deep site (with few categories, but many subcategories). Then map out your site structure by categorising your content into top level categories and subcategories. Use your site map and storyboards to help in this task.

I recently advised on the development of a musical instrument website that sells wind, string and percussion instruments. There were lengthy discussions about the category of some instruments, as to whether to place them in a wind or brass section and whether the accessories that accompanied the instruments should be grouped together on one page or placed beneath the instrument pages.

To help in the organisation of your own website's information, check your categorisation with a target group and observe their surfing methods and habits. Ask the group to complete a questionnaire to provide valuable feedback on their own experience of finding information on your website.

2.9 Meta-Tags

Meta-tags are a general purpose tag that you can utilise to include information about the page you have designed. Information about the author, contact details, and a description about the page are all acceptable types of tags. The majority of search engines will use these meta-tags to help index your web pages and site, so getting them right is important.

Developers spend an enormous amount of time experimenting with meta-tags and analysing what keywords work and which ones don't.

The first tag you should include in your web page is the title:

```
<html><head><title>Cleaning Company</title></head>
```

Two of the most important meta-tags are the 'description' and 'keywords' tag. They look something like this:

```
<meta name="description"
content="Feedback form for cleaning company." />
```

```
<meta name="keywords"
content="cleaning, clean, wipe, wash, detergent" />
```

The 'description' tag provides the search engine with an accurate description of your web page and using the second tag of keywords, allows the search engine to index your page based upon these words. It is a good idea to consider mis-spelt words in addition to the correctly spelt versions just in case users may get the search phrase or word wrong.

If your website contains a discussion forum then it is a good idea to include a tag to exclude those particular pages from being indexed. There is nothing more annoying than seeing hundreds of pages in a search listing with nothing but user responses in a discussion room. Use the following to exclude a page from being indexed:

<meta name="robots" content="noindex">

Meta-tags can be a very useful tool for other purposes other than just identifying your web page to search engines. I could probably write a short book just on meta-tags and code associated with it. However to show you one more use for meta-tags as evidence of their usefulness, a tag can be used to place a time limit on the viewing of a web page:

<meta http-equiv="refresh" content="10;URL=nextpage.htm" />

This will make any page automatically load another page after a pre-defined amount of time, in this particular case, 10 seconds. Replace the 'nextpage.htm' with your choice of page to load.

Useful resources:

Webdeveloper.com
www.webdeveloper.com/html/html_metatags.html

Meta Tag Analyser Tool
www.widexl.com/remote/search-engines/metatag-analyzer.html

Part 3
Managing
Your Website

3.1 Deploying Your Website

Once your website is ready for the public, it needs to be uploaded to a web server. To reiterate, choosing who is going to host your site is an important decision. For success, your website needs to be available twenty four hours a day, seven days a week. Any 'down-time' could lose you potential revenue, not to mention frustrate visitors.

Steps for deployment of your site onto the web include:

- **Register your Domain Name.**
Register your domain name as soon as possible. The design of your website may be centred round it.

- **Investigate a suitable Web Host.**
Set-up your website's hosting either through your own infrastructure or an account with a reputable internet service provider.

- **Upload your web pages to the Web Server.**
Set up directories or folders on the web server following the structure you designed earlier. You may need to set up FTP (file transfer protocol) access on your computer to upload files and content.

- **Transfer Data to Web Server.**
Copy the files through a FTP connection onto the web server but don't upload your site until it's complete. 'Under Construction' pages don't create a good impression.

- **Configure any required scripts on the Web Server.**
Scripts can be used for all kinds of tasks, from accepting input from the user through to a form to convert data into an email.

All these scripts need to be uploaded to the web server and configured ensuring that you have the right permissions set for access. Alternatively you may use scripts provided by your host and so you'll need to check the path to the scripts is correct.

- **Test your Website.**

Test functionality as well as the look and feel in a variety of different browsers and hardware environments. Get feedback from a small test group of users. Check for any broken links or orphaned files. Macromedia Dreamweaver, one of the most popular packages for producing professional websites, does this for you automatically and produces a detailed report.

Useful Resource:

Macromedia Dreamweaver
www.macromedia.com/software/dreamweaver

3.2 Managing Your Website

Once your website is out there, you need to manage it effectively. The task is a complex one and covers a range of areas and topics as I mentioned at the beginning. The main difference I have found between managing a website business to any other business is the rapid speed at which events develop and change. Floods of emails can suddenly appear in your inbox and everybody expects a quick reply. At one time, a week was considered normal for a response to a postal enquiry. Now an email response is expected within the day if not sooner.

It takes many years of experience, training and commercial insight to gain a full understanding of all the attributes needed to successfully accomplish the task of website management.

However, I hope this section will provide you with some introductory information that you can apply to your own websites.

Monitor and Analyse Site Traffic

Know how your site is being used by its visitors. Your internet service provider or hosting provider should give you access to reports about the usage of your site, where the traffic originated from, and what types of browsers visitors were using. Various companies offer more sophisticated analysis tools as part of their hosting package.

Update Content

Keep your site content up-to-date and constantly provide new information. Providing a good resource for information will keep your visitors returning to your website. Review on a regular basis whether you should add more information to popular sections.

Verify and Update Links

Ensure links to external websites are working, although realise that this is out of your control to a large extent. Constant checking is necessary. Pages and even sites can change or disappear. Avoid visitor frustration by keeping links up-to-date all the time.

Respond to Visitors' Feedback

Your website's visitors are a great resource for ideas on how to improve your site. Providing a feedback page can be an avenue for users to air their ideas.

Deal with Technical Issues

Even the best website hosted by the best ISP will suffer from the occasional hiccup. Several years ago, I was involved in a training programme for a well known high street computer store training their staff in technical support. Their extreme strategy when dealing with customer's technical issues had been to first suggest rebooting the computer and re-installing Windows! This was common practice to avoid admitting to customers that the fault was on the part of the ISP. This, I'm pleased to say, has changed in more recent times with better technical support being offered and the availability of more highly skilled second-line support. This illustrates the importance of making sure that you secure the knowledge to deal with technical issues efficiently and effectively.

3.3 Promoting and Marketing

Even the best website is worthless if nobody visits it. To ensure a constant flow of visitors, it is advisable to promote the site as thoroughly as possible. This should be done as an ongoing process just as with other businesses. Search engines are probably the first port of call for promoting your website. Magazines often feature reviews of submitted websites and can generate traffic. Web banners on other sites that advertise your own site and will direct traffic to you are usually a useful method of promotion.

Let's look at some of the ways you can promote your website:

Search Engine Optimization

To ensure you are indexed with all the search engines, each web page should be optimised. Carrying out this task will ensure you get a good position in the listings. Ensure all your meta-tags are complete and contain adequate information. Having external links within your website will increase ranking with search engines.

Register with all the appropriate Search Engines

Consider individual registration with the major search engines and possible mass registration with smaller engines and directories. Look for any search engines that specialise in specific fields or topics that may be relevant to your website topic.

Industry Directory Listings

Many industries have their own directories where you can find their products, suppliers or local dealerships. Submit your website to companies that specialise in your product or service area.

Banner Advertising

Advertise your site on other websites, which are visited by your target audience. This can be costly but effective with the right audience. Use the LinkExchange banner network or purchase banner ads. Make sure your target market demographics match that of the site hosting your banner ads.

Exchanging Links with other Websites

Exchanging links with other websites is a great way of getting your website known. It is a cheap and cost effect way of advertising and increases your ratings with the search engines. This method is very similar to banner advertising.

Site Sponsoring

Sponsoring lends credibility in addition to giving you exposure. Often you can sponsor content on another web site. Gorp.com is an example of an outdoor sponsorship site. Again make sure your target market demographics match.

Integration of Website and Print Media

Once your website is complete, use your print media to direct your customers to your website. Your website should not replace print media, but work in conjunction with it. Submit your website to magazines for review. Maybe they'll write a feature on you!

Use Traditional Media

Advertise your web site just like you would advertise a product or service using print adverts, directory listings, trade publications, radio, television or bill boards.

Use Pay-Per-Click Adverts

Well-targeted pay-per-click adverts, such as Google Adwords, can considerably increase your site's traffic and business. Research thoroughly or invest in hiring a specialist in this area.

Your Publicity Materials

Include your web address on business cards, letterheads, envelopes, catalogues and brochures. Any material that leaves your office with your name on it, should also include your web address.

Set-up Email Signatures

Make sure that you and any employees sign email messages with complete names and company contact information including your web address. Most email programs can automatically insert this information for you.

Direct Mail

Notify friends, family, colleagues and clients of your new website and whenever you make significant changes. Consider an email newsletter or periodic email to keep your name in front of your clients. Remember that SPAM – sending unsolicited email – is illegal and could have serious implications so make sure that you have an 'opt-in' email list!

Indexing and Linking

Most people find your website by clicking a link found on another website. Develop links from as many websites as possible and consider some of the following pointers:

- When you register with search engines, you can often register more than just your homepage. Sites with extensive information should register gateway pages into different sections.
- Use announcement services and newsgroups. Use these services appropriately. You can find appropriate newsgroups by searching at www.dejanews.com.
- Research links in industry/topical directories.
- Seek links from associations and business groups.
- Look for links from local and regional directories.
- Locate links from complementary websites - suppliers, manufacturers and clients.

Pay-per-Click and Online Advertising

Internet marketing and online advertising is expected to pass the $7.2billion mark by 2007. I have noticed that more search engines are now charging for submissions. Until now search engines have survived on advertising. This is no longer the case as competition heats up.

PPC (Pay-per-Click) and SEO (search engine optimisation) are the most effective ways of targeting visitors to a website. If you aren't taking advantage of this then you can be sure your competitors are.

Benefits of Pay-per-Click include:

- Instant website traffic – no waiting months for results.
- Only pay for actual click-throughs, not impressions.
- PPC results are predictable and stable. You know where you stand.
- ROI (Return on investment) for PPC is very good, one of the best in advertising.
- Low risk, only pay for the website traffic you get.

More on Banner Ads

Banner Ads are becoming less popular as their effectiveness decreases. They are probably the most commonly known form of web advertising around, however click through rates are not that good. More sophisticated forms of advertising are now available that allow you to advertise but don't cost you as much or anything at all unless you actually generate a sale. I still like the use of banner advertising. It's simple and easy to implement, but in a commercial environment, it's not as effective as some of the alternatives.

Affiliate Programs

Associate and affiliate programs are big business on the internet, but few realise that they have progressed far beyond the original concept that was introduced by the likes of Amazon.com

An affiliate program (sometimes termed an Associate Program) allows companies to advertise on websites other than their own. You could sell your products and services on other websites by setting up an affiliate scheme. This is an effective way of increasing traffic and your affiliates gain a commission on sales.

Many websites make money by including affiliate links on their own sites and get paid commission on results. It doesn't cost you anything to sign-up to an affiliate program. Enter `Free Affiliate programs' in to any search engine and you'll find a long list available.

Useful Resources:

Affiliate Programs
Commission Junction - www.cj.com

Paying for Search Engine Inclusion

As I said earlier, the days of free search engines submission is fast declining. Search engines have had to look elsewhere as internet advertising revenues decrease. Most are now running the pay for inclusions (PFI) program. This means that you pay a set amount for each URL for quick inclusion into the search engine database. However, a good ranking position is not guaranteed. Your site will still need to be optimised to achieve the best results.

Let's look at the benefits for the pay-for-inclusion system:

- Quick inclusion into the database. The process takes around a week.

- The site will be included in the database for as long as the subscription is maintained. There is no dropping of the website due to a change in the algorithm or other changes.

- The website will receive repeated 'spidering' every 48 hours, giving you plenty of opportunities to enhance any pages required. This method allows you the chance to see what changes may cause low or high rankings.

For larger sites and especially ecommerce ones, I recommend paying for your inner sales pages to be included. Home pages will be indexed for free eventually.

Examples of Pay for Inclusion search engines are:

INKTOMI

Inktomi provides search engine technology that powers other search partners. One of its bigger partners is MSN. Submission will appear in:

- Hotbot
- About.com
- Overture
- MSN
- Looksmart
- Terra.com

- Soneraplaza
- Bluewin
- Blueyonder
- And more...

ALTAVISTA

It is possible to get AltaVista to index your website for free, but you will have to wait about three months. To get listed faster, you will have to pay. Instead of an annual subscription, AltaVista offers a six monthly subscription period that is renewable every six months. Inclusion is within seven days and spidering takes place every 48 hours.

Search Term Advertising

Most search engines will offer advertising based on the search term which is used. For example, if you were a computer retailer your advert would be shown on a search for 'computer software' but not for 'television repairs'. This is very effective at increasing your click-through-rate, which is especially important as most of these systems are based on pay-for-views, not pay-per-click. They are cost effective and are a good way of mounting a medium scale advertising campaign.

3.4　Search Engine Analysis and Optimisation

SEO (Search Engine Optimisation) is a business and skill in itself. There are many tools around on the internet that claim to substantially increase your business if you buy their SEO software, however, there are cheaper methods that will certainly assist in the task and won't cost a fortune.

A good knowledge and understanding of how the search engines work means that you can optimise your website and tailor it to make it search engine friendly. However, once indexed by the search engines, it is essential that you monitor the performance and analyse the search engine results.

Here are some SEO terms and phrases to familiarise yourself with:

- **Search engine optimisation (SEO).**
SEO is about optimising your web content to make the web pages attractive and visible so that they are picked by the search engines.

- **Search engine results page (SERP).**
Are listings or results, displayed for a particular search.

- **Search engine marketing (SEM).**
As well as using SEO techniques, SEM more frequently refers to marketing of a website to search engines through paid placements and adverts.

- **Directory.**
A directory is a human-compiled search. Most directories rely on submission instead of spiders.

- **Keywords, keyterms, and keyphrases.**
These are words you want your web site to rank well in the SERPS (search engine results pages).

- **Link farm.**
In SEO, a link farm is a page full of links that have very little to do with each other and exist just as links without any real content.

- **Organic listings.**

These are free listings in the SERPs. This usually involves improving the actual content of your website.

- **PageRank.**

Is a measure that the Google-obsessed use to test their rankings.

- **Paid listing.**

Depending on the search engine, a paid listing represents paying for your website or page to be included into an index, a pay per click (PPC) advert, or a sponsored link. Other methods also exist to get your website into the SERPs for targeted keywords and phrases.

- **Ranking.**

A ranking is where your page is listed in the SERPs for your targeted keywords.

- **Ranking algorithm.**

This is a set of rules that a search engine uses to evaluate and rank the listings in its index.

- **Spamming.**

This is a method of optimisation that attempts to trick a spider into indexing your website through exploiting loopholes in the ranking algorithm.

- **Spider.**

A spider crawls through the web looking for listings to add to a search engine index. It is sometimes referred to as a webcrawler or robot.

There are several simple measurements that you can make that will provide a wealth of information about your customers wants and needs. You should be tracking what your users are searching for, how many results they may have got through the search and how many of the users bought something that they had searched for.

Some ways to analyse the results:

Search Phrases

Analysing your search phrase results can reveal patterns that may help you spot problem areas. Keeping track of frequently used search phrases and keywords typed incorrectly may point to possible fixes that will be required. Using various spelling options for a product name may help visitors locate the goods with greater ease. Zero results searches can also point out problematic areas in your website navigation. Analysing searching techniques may indicate whether customers are searching for products by product description, vendor type, or model number. Try to match your descriptions to the search results. Your website must use the same language as your customers.

Missed Opportunities

If your customers are searching for items that you don't carry, it can point out missed sales opportunities. Try to spot these and then maybe adapt your sales catalogue to include these products.

Interface Problems

Your analysis report can also point out user interface problems. How often do users search for blank strings or the default search value? i.e. you have "Enter text here" as the default string in the search box.

Popular Search Terms

Look at the most popular search terms and reflect on why they are the most popular. Is that item fashionable right now? Consider the popular search phrases that provide a large number of results. The chances are that a large number of choices will overload the customers, however you should consider using these phrases for headers for the various categories in your product listings. Laying the categories out clearly will help the customers find what they are looking for and make a sale much quicker.

Check your Navigation

Are your users having a tough time finding a product? Place a link to that product on the home page or otherwise promote it in a more visible manner to help your sales.

Tracking Conversion Rates

Tracking the conversion rate of the searches will provide you with some very useful feedback on how effective your sales strategy is. If the conversion rate is low then your prices are too high or the sales copy needs to be adjusted. Customers are looking for specific products and will assume the search results have pointed them to the right one. If this is the case then the conversion rate will be quite high.

3.5 Attracting and Retaining your Website's Visitors

Gaining and retaining visitors to your website is all about giving people what they want. Basic information about your organisation or service is great, but after reading it once, what will encourage your visitor to return to your site?

To make your website stand out from the competition, you need to find a need in your target audience and provide a solution. Compared to other media, the costs of internet development are low. It takes only a short amount of time and little resources to provide your visitors with a better web experience.

Consider the following ideas:

Inspired Purchases

If your website sells products or services then your aim is to inspire purchases. If you sell furniture then try offering your users a design tool for planning the layout of a room or articles on the best bedroom or kitchen designs. Extra tools such as this prove to be beneficial features.

Feature Product Reviews

Product reviews are always a good inclusion on a web page. You are much more likely to sell your inventory if you offer reviews of the products you are selling. Persuade your customers to write reviews, hire experts to write them or syndicate product reviews from a third party.

Provide Useful Tools

Consider offering tools that make the visitors tasks easier such as calculators, calendars or response forms. Having a mortgage or loan calculator on a web page can encourage visitors to bookmark your page. I have several websites bookmarked on my favourites because of a currency exchange calculator features on a web page or a savings account interest calculator.

Offer Freebies

Everybody loves free gifts, so offer graphics, ebooks, back-issues of your publication, recipes, patterns or plans depending on the type of site you offer.

Run Competitions

Contests are always popular so consider how you can implement this into your website. Remember to look into the legalities of running a competition and ensure that you have well-worded rules and conditions of entry.

Provide Expert Information

Hire a subject expert for your website. This will give your visitors access to professional information.

Update your Content

Your visitors will return if you regularly update your content. Include fresh articles on a regular basis to keep your website fresh. Provide technical specifications for your products.

Include a Blog

Blogging is the latest and most addictive tool for capturing an attentive web audience. This involves writing a regular `diary' type entry on your website or linked to a specialist blog website. If you have the right subject, you can attract a large amount of traffic on a regular basis.

Offer a Free Email Facility

Even if you don't own a domain, you can still offer email through several services. If you do own a domain, even better!

Whenever the person wants to check their mail, they have to return to your site to login. Take a look at: www.everyone.net or www.bigmailbox.com.

Offer a Discussion Forum

A discussion forum is a useful tool and once you've got it going, people will return to check if anybody has responded to their posts or to read the latest threads. The forums will need moderating though to keep content under control. You can easily run one if you have CGI and Perl access on your web host. If you would rather have a remotely hosted message board, take a look at www.groupee.com.

Any or all of these ideas can be easily implemented and will pay dividends in making your website successful. Keep in mind that if you have more than one target audience, you might engage several strategies for gaining and keeping visitors.

3.6 Understanding your Website's Visitors

During the summer I spent many hours with a colleague looking through statistics and information on who was visiting her website. It is very interesting to see the visitor's country of origin, time of day when they visit and what pages they view. All this information will help you understand your site's visitors so that you can revise your website to suit.

There are many methods and varying pieces of software available to monitor the visitors to your website. The type of information you can obtain includes:

- Number of visitors and page-views in any time period.
- Predicted numbers of visitors and page-views.
- ISP and domain name of visitors.
- Visitor's country.
- Amount of time visitors spend on site.
- Entry page - First page they saw on your site.
- Exit page - Last page they saw on your site.
- Referring page - The last page visitors were on before yours.
- The visitor's browser.
- The visitor's IP address.

Traffic Analysis

There are different ways to measure success for web sites so choose one that fits with the purpose of your site. Some of the information used to evaluate success, such as number of visitors or number of hits, will come from analyzing the server log files for your website. By using log files, you can find out which sites are linking to you, what words and phrases were used by search engines to find you and what pages visitors viewed.

Analysing the traffic to your website is an effective method of deducing your site's performance. Some of the traffic data points that you should analyse are:

- Look at the number of visitors to your website.
- Consider how many repeat visitors you have returning to your site.
- Analyse what pages were viewed by your visitors. This is sometimes called the number of hits.
- Review the sales and marketing leads generated compared to actual sales of products or services.

- Monitor the number of information requests you receive.
- Look at visitor feedback and see if any patterns or repeating comments occur.
- Consider whether the number of client support calls have reduced as this will decrease your expenses.
- Monitor the visitor details that are left on your site.

Site Counters

The most common, but least informative way to look at traffic is to track hits or page views. This is what counters at the bottom of web pages do. However, this is not the same as the number of people viewing your web page. A count is recorded every time a visitor loads or reloads a page. For example: if a visitor starts on the homepage, goes to another page and then comes back to the homepage, the counter will show two hits. As you can see, one visitor can generate lots of hits. And to complicate matters, that visitor might be you. Many people check their own web pages regularly without realizing that their visits are boosting the hit counter.

Server Log Files

A much better way to track website traffic is to analyze your server log files. Every time someone visits your website, your web server records what they looked at, for how long, what browser they used, what kind of computer they have, what they downloaded, which website they came from, and even what keywords they used at a search engine to find your site. All this information is compiled into a log file and can be mined for important demographic data and traffic trends.

The log records every single page, image and script request and will record information about the computer which makes the request, if it was successful and how much data was transferred. Check your hosting package to see what information is available. If however you have built your own web server and placed it online then you have all the information at your finger tips.

Once you have the log file you need to download a program or script which will analyse the file and display the information on the screen. There are many of these which all do different things with the data. To find one, search for Log File Analysers. Some hosts will automatically generate statistics from your log files online.

Using an Online Questionnaire

Even from the detailed information you can gain from web server logs, it is still difficult to really get to know your visitors and there is only one sure way of finding out more about them. If you create a members only section on your website then you can have a questionnaire for people to complete which then provides access to that section of the site. This may annoy some people but if you keep the questionnaire brief and relevant, it will glean some informative results.

How to Use the Information

Once you start analysing your log files, you find out which pages in your site are generating traffic and which ones aren't. Use this information to rework content and navigation to promote pages that aren't receiving traffic. Or, remove pages that aren't of interest to your audience.

Use the visitor browser information to gauge the types of technology that your visitors can handle, and design your web pages accordingly.

Check the visitor demographics. This may help you refine the content you provide. Tailoring your content to those cultures or countries may boost ratings.

Website Promotion Tips

To reiterate on the main points, here are some tips that won't break the bank but could effectively promote your website:

- List your website with the big search engines and directories first.

- Make sure your website is optimised for the search engines. This includes adding meta-tags and making sure you have all the keywords, titles and descriptions in place.

- Send out email newsletters to your opt-in list promoting your website and the launch. Encourage people to visit your site possibly by giving away a free gift to the first hundred users.

- Join an online discussion group or newsgroup and get involved. Taking up a discussion page on www.about.com gives you an opportunity to mention your website and circulate your name as an authority on a product or subject topic.

- Place your URL everywhere.

- Place a signature on all your emails.

- Exchange links with other websites and companies.

- Send out press releases to magazines. Positive reviews can build success. This is how Ebay started.

- Offer free gifts. Everybody loves a free gift and it encourages traffic to your website.

- Offer loyalty rewards. Give discount coupons to users that revisit your site.

3.7 Good Communication

Email Response Times

How many times have you visited a website and then had trouble attempting to locate contact details or an email address? Then, if you are successful at locating the contact information, you send an email but never get a reply? I am sure you all relate to my own frustration in this matter.

Email is an essential part of your website strategy. It forms part of the quality of service you as an individual or part of a company offer to your clients and customers. Part of your mission statement may state that all emails will be answered within a set period of time. Automated responses could form part of this mission statement.

Professional Email

The email address structure you use also forms part of the business image you portray to your website visitors.

Many years ago when I started out in the web business an associate was impressed that I had an email address at a domain name that was not part of a known ISP. e.g.: Phil@mycompany.com. Most people had hotmail accounts or an email address at btinternet.co.uk for example but to own an email address at your own domain name demonstrated another level of professionalism and commitment towards your business.

Whenever you purchase a domain name, it is likely you will also get email opportunities available with the domain name. Apart from the usual personal email addresses, you will have the opportunity to create less personal ones such as Director@owncompany.com or Admin@yourcompany.co.uk

The email addresses you create through the domain name are only a front. They are not direct mail boxes that you hold access to through your ISP or on your own web server. It is quite likely that you will already hold an email address with your ISP and therefore what is required is a forwarding link created from the domain name email address and the current ISP email address that you hold. When an email is sent to you the message is forwarded from the created email address through to you at your ISP. To respond to the user with the same email address requires you to amend the outgoing email address in your email program, such as Outlook. You must maintain the existing outgoing email server name as this is the one used by your ISP and cannot be changed. However, outgoing email servers don't usually authenticate the outgoing email address name and so any outgoing message you send will be delivered to the recipient with the chosen email address for your company. To a large extent you could call it an email spoof.

Your Contact Details

Contact details are sometimes difficult to locate on many websites. This is usually because the webmaster doesn't want you to contact them through any other method than maybe their feedback or enquiry form. Postal addresses and telephone numbers are usually near impossible to locate. My advice to you as a web developer is to consider carefully your method of communication. Being inundated by emails is okay if you can handle a suitable reply within an acceptable response time. Feedback or enquiry forms are useful as they collect only relevant information that you want and you can format the layout so that the data is easily and quickly processed. Try placing instructions on your website as to what method of communication you prefer. Your visitors may not always follow it though. How you deal with your communications will provide visitors with an indication of your professionalism.

3.8 Security Issues

Spyware, Trojans, Adware and Scumware

The majority of computer users are aware of the darker side of the internet. Being online brings issues of credit card fraud, identity theft, junk-mail, spam and seedy content right to our desktop in our homes. But how many of you are unwitting accomplices to this?

Your computer could, without your knowledge, be used to send spam, capture email addresses, and launch denial of service (DoS) attacks on networks or systems around the web. Denial of service attacks can crash a whole system by inundating its servers with HTTP requests. A recent audit of over one million computers revealed 29.5 million instances of spyware, which is an average of 28 spyware items on each computer.

How does this happen without your knowledge? Examples like those mentioned earlier are the work of Trojans. These are small programs that can be unknowingly installed on a computer and then accessed by other computers through the internet. Spyware, adware, viruses and Trojans are all collectively known as "malware" or "pestware". While the majority of such programs are pests and nothing more, they have the potential to be quite nasty.

Trojans

Trojans do not replicate like some viruses but they do carry a hidden piece of code within them that embeds itself on a computer and then allows another computer to contact it. A trojan can take control of a computer. Trojans are known as RATS. (Remote Access Trojans). They are hidden within many downloads on the internet such as games and music download software.

Spyware

Spyware programs vary from simple keyboard logging programs to more dangerous ones that capture personal data such as passwords and usernames. Again spyware can be hidden within downloads, but most commonly they are packaged with shareware or freeware.

Legitimate applications can legally contain spyware. Such programs are marketed as tools for keeping tabs on children and spouses online. One program called Activity Logger, for example, connects to the internet on its own, records the URLs of sites visited and the keystrokes from email and chat applications. It will also capture screenshots that can be made into a slide show.

Adware

Adware, or advertisement ware, are programs that display advertisements on your computer. They can be part of other software or come bundled within an application. Adware is usually not malicious although it can be irritating. Some adware can collect sim information such as IP addresses.

Viruses

Viruses are a potentially lethal piece of software that can destroy a computer and its software and data. Over 60% of businesses that suffer a major virus attack do not fully recover. Email viruses are probably the most common and are easily delivered to the heart of users and innocently opened and activated. Email is also the perfect tool for the spread of viruses within an organisation and across the internet.

It is said that viruses cost employers hundreds of millions of pounds each year. The infection of a web server or website could put a business down for hours or days leading to lost revenue. The installation of a Firewall and Virus protection software help prevent attacks but not completely.

The MS Blaster worm that caused havoc in the summer of 2003 exploited a vulnerability in the Remote Procedure Call (RPC) function of the Windows Operating System. Nearly all those that did not have a patch that was issued by Microsoft fell foul of the worm. This marked a new era in virus prevention for many computer users. Taking care with email attachments was no longer sufficient to keep you safe.

Is your Computer Infected?

Spyware, trojans and other viruses contact other computers; they use system resources such as CPU cycles, memory and an internet connection which will slow your computer's performance. A sudden change in how your computer is running could be a sign of spyware or adware.

If you're getting a lot of bounced back email and see evidence of emails being sent without your knowledge, then it's possible that trojan spamware has found its way onto your computer. Spamware is a trojan that can turn your computer into a spam launching pad and create headaches for unknowing computer users, especially if a virus is sent. Even if your computer is not being used to send spam, trojans can steal a copy of your email address book and send it back to a spammer.

Scumware

Scumware, in case you haven't yet heard of it, is a webmaster's worst nightmare! Imagine a program which could place links on your site which you didn't want, such as links to your competitors, links to pornography and changes to your advertisements so that they don't earn you any money. Several years ago this would have been impossible, but not anymore.

Scumware is downloaded with other software applications or it comes bundled with other software. Scumware scans and identifies keywords within the webpage and then attaches itself to the code. Banner adverts are routed out and replaced with other adverts not of your choosing and so removing any revenue you may earn from them. Although the site code doesn't actually alter the website it merely adds links to the advertisements and redirects them. There are legal implications to this type of software in terms of copyright.

There is code on the internet that can help block scumware. If you have a search for `scumware blockers' then you will find a suitable list. But beware of the adware, spyware, trojans and scumware that may be contained within these!

Removal of Malicious Programs

Removal of spyware or viruses is a tricky procedure that is too complex and complicated to explain in this brief section. It requires a degree of expertise and knowledge of the workings of the software so I suggest leaving the removal task to a professional. There are a number of applications available that will do the task for you.

Where spyware is concerned, there is some advice I can offer and that is before any removal or remedy is applied you should unplug your computer from the internet. No remedy can be applied while you are connected to your ISP, and remember if you advertise your email address everywhere then you can expect to receive loads of attention. It's a little like standing in a city centre and shouting your telephone number through a megaphone. Don't be surprised if somebody phones you!

Phishing

This is one of the latest scams on the internet. Phishing is also referred to as brand spoofing or carding. The phrase was coined in 1996 by hackers who stole AOL internet accounts by scamming passwords from unsuspecting AOL users. The "f' was replaced by "ph" as is so common with hackers and so the term phishing was born. It involves a user falsely claiming to be an organisation in an attempt to defraud another user out of money or information that can lead to losing money. The scam usually starts off by sending an email containing falsely acquired graphics and asking for the victim to follow a link to a website and enter bank details or account information.

In January 2006, nearly 18,000 reports of phishing were made to the Anti-Phishing Work Group (APWG), with 101 brands hijacked by phishing campaigns. The United States was the country hosting the most phishing websites. Each site is online for an average of five days before closing and moving on. APWG has available a large amount of statistical data about phishing and is well worth a visit.

One of the most memorable and recent incidents was a phishing scam in which users supposedly received emails from Ebay claiming that the user's account was about to be suspended unless he or she clicked on the provided link and updated the credit card information that was already held by Ebay. The clickable link that users were asked to follow would point to a website that simulates the original in every detail with graphics stolen from the original organisation, and content in all the right places so as to make the site look genuine and legitimate. The scam works by conning the user into thinking the site they are redirected to is genuine.

How to spot a scam

It is not always easy to spot a scam at first glance; many people can go into panic-mode when they read the email usually stating a consequence for not following the link. It must be stated that while the source email address may exist, the email has not originated from that address; this is what is known as a spoof email. In fact nearly anybody can send one of these. I once sent one to a friend in the US on her birthday from TheQueen@buckinghampalace.co.uk I don't think that address is genuine though!

Within the email there will be a clickable link that you are supposed to follow. If you highlight the clickable link, the IP address should be displayed within the browser. You can check this IP address against the genuine IP address of the company. In some instances the phisher may replace the link 'Click Here' with an actual URL address like www.amazon/accounts to make the link look more genuine.

In addition to checking the link, look for spelling mistakes and logos that don't look the exact size or quality to the original.

The Phisher

Anyone who has an email address is likely to be a potential victim to phishing at some point. If you have published an email address on a chat room, discussion forum, bulletin board or newsgroup, then it is likely that your email address could be on a hit list. Spiders crawl the internet logging email addresses from these kinds of sites and then the scam artists access these logs cheaply and easily giving them access to millions of valid email addresses to send these scams to.

How to avoid a scam

One piece of advice that I can offer is do not click on any links from an email you are sent. No one ever asks for personal information like account or card details within an email. Delete the email immediately. If possible check your emails through web mail as opposed to downloading them in Outlook as this will minimise the potential of infecting your computer from a virus should an email contain one.

If you are still not convinced about the legitimacy of the email and think there may be an issue concerning an account then close the email and browser and reopen a new browser window and type in the genuine URL to visit the site and follow the links within it. Do not use the 'click here' or 'follow this link' within the email.

If you receive a phishing email then depending on where you live, you can report this to the Federal Trade Commission (FTC) or some other local authority that deals with Internet Anti-Phishing.

Useful Resources:

Anti-Phishing Working Group
www.antiphishing.org

3.9 Disaster Recovery - What are your plans?

Giving some thought to how you may recover from various disasters that might befall you is not such a bad idea. Although war is not covered by insurance companies, flood, fire, and hurricanes may affect your business. However, some simpler problems are more easily avoidable. Here are some likely ones that may befall you:

- The hard drive dies on your web server. It is completely unrecoverable and all the data has disappeared.

- Your host or ISP goes out of business; they experience a fire or flood and their computers are no longer working.

- Some novice hacker attempts to break through your security fence and play around with your website.

- Your business partner takes off to the sun with the passwords to all your web servers and accounts. Do you know the passwords to your website? Does more than one person know how to do the updates?

You should have a solid back-up plan in place. Documentation should exist in more than one location.

Some years back when I worked for a computer services department in a construction company, I was required to drive to various locations around the city placing back-up copies of the week's data in fire proof safes for security.

Having a back-up of your website is equally important as any data. In addition, you should have copies of database content, clients' personal information and copies of orders placed together with email accounts of everyone within your organisation. You may have to restore these at some point.

Control of your Site

If you have to move your website to another machine, perhaps at another ISP, you will need to update the name servers that point users at your website. You may have used a redirection service; if so, you need to amend the details. Ensuring you have access to all the site and usernames is essential. It is sometimes common practice for web development companies to maintain this information on your behalf. If you become unhappy with their service and change to another company, getting this information can be difficult.

Keep a portfolio of the essential information needed to manage and run your website. Updating the top level domain servers can take between 24 and 48 hours for all the changes to take effect. If you have to wait for your web developer to get round to doing the job for you, then your website could be down for a week or more.

Even a simple brochure type website consisting of a few HTML pages can cause problems if it's down for any length of time. You need to keep control of your site and domain name.

Copies of the HTML files

Do you have copies of all your website's files as a back-up? This includes HTML pages, the images and all of the files that comprise your website. It's all very well if your ISP does network back-ups. However, you won't have access to those back-ups if the ISP has gone bankrupt. Make sure you have your own copy as well.

In my case, I have a development web server in my study. I make all of the website changes there before uploading them to the public server, so I have a back-up copy built into my process. If you don't do this, or if you pay someone else to develop your website for you, make sure you get updates. Using CD or DVD are good ways to generate a spare copy.

Database Back-Ups

The data within the database is always changing, so a monthly back-up usually isn't sufficient. Personally, the database on my website is set-up to allow remote access. So every night, I pull a complete copy of the data down to the development server in my study. The most I'll lose is a single days worth of data which is an acceptable risk to me. Allowing remote access is a security hole though, so some web hosts won't do it. One of my customers has a script that runs on their web server every eight hours. It dumps a copy of the database contents and emails it to their home account. Note that the email address you send the database back-up to should not be on the same server as your website. If the web server is down, you can't get at the email either.

A list of Usernames, Passwords and Special Programs

If you own or lease your own web server, you probably have other software installed on it that you can't easily find on the average web host. This might be mailing list software, special scripts or scheduled tasks. Make sure you have a copy of the source code for every one of these programs. You'll need them to rebuild the website on a new server. This includes license numbers for shopping carts, merchant accounts, FTP programs, everything that goes into making the website tick.

If you have multiple employees, you should know all of their account names on the web server. If you need to set these up again on another server, having that list is really useful. If you have separate mailing list software, are there any special mail server configurations that would need to be set-up again?

Your disaster recovery plan needs to be tailored to your website's requirements. Larger companies have the cash to solve this problem by running two copies of their website, often on opposite sides of the country. If you're going to pay to have two copies of the website, you might as well use both of them instead of leaving the spare collecting dust in a storage room. It's more cost effective and everybody will forget to update the spare if it's not being used frequently. For the rest of us with smaller budgets, we need to have a plan to rebuild. Just remember, a disaster is only an emergency if you're not prepared for it. Over 60% of organisations that suffer a computer system crash never fully recover.

Automate your 404 Errors

From time to time it is good practice to review the error log produced by your web server. The log will quickly point out many of the places on your site where errors exist and that you missed during the testing stage. Visitors are very quick to find faults and errors and if broken links exist, they will leave the site and find another. Maintaining the functionality of your site is very important.

The main problem is that once the website is live, you will be busy updating various pages. The task of checking for any broken links quite often gets shoved to the back of the queue, so far back that it never gets looked at.

The 404 error is the web server error code for `Page Not Found'. We've all run up against this a time or two. It's a good idea to create a custom 404 page, which will preserve the look and feel of your website and reassure your visitors that they haven't completely left your site. It is a good idea to place notes or hints on your pages if you move any of the content to a new location. These hints will point the user to the new destination and avoid frustration developing. Building a custom 404 page will also keep visitors informed of any changes made to your website. Should you combine both concepts, the custom 404 page and reviewing the error log, you should be able to gain quick feedback on any broken links or pages.

Most web servers will be able to run some kind of scripting language, be it PHP, ASP, ColdFusion or Perl. Always attempt to write your 404 and 500 error pages in one of those kinds of scripts and have it send an email to you or your webmaster if an error is encountered. The basis of this scheme can actually produce more work for you as any errors on your site will then generate email. This can be quite annoying but it will prompt you or your webmaster to promptly fix the site. It means you can fix problems quickly and it will be done much sooner than if you waited until the next review of the error log file.

Most modern email programs like Outlook have filters or rules that allow you to automatically route incoming emails into particular folders based on the subject header or sender. These emails can be directed to individuals around the organisation or just to folders that can be accessed by specific individuals. Ignoring these emails can be detrimental to your business so don't allow them to be deposited into a folder within the depths of the hard drive and just forgotten about. Setting up a policy or procedure is only effective if it is followed.

If you want to go all out on this theme, you can create a custom page for just about every type of server error code available. Error 500 is another one that is probably useful to trap like this and I'll talk about that next. Still 404 is the most common error on a website so fixing that first is recommended.

Error 500

Error 500 means your web server encountered an unexpected condition that prevented it from fulfilling the request by the client for access to the requested URL.

This is a 'catch-all' error generated by your web server. It means something has happened but the server cannot be more specific about the error condition in its response to the client.

In addition to the 500 error being notified back to the client, the web server will most likely generate an entry in the internal error log which gives more details of what went wrong. It is up to you or your webmaster to locate and analyse the logs.

This error can only be resolved by fixes to the web server software. It rarely has any bearing on the actual web page or website. It is not a client-side problem and so has nothing to do with the browser. If you ever encounter an error 500, email the webmaster and inform them of the circumstances that led to the error.

3.10 Web Server Software

Any computer can be made into a web server; however software is required to make the html pages available to the client or user and to control the flow of information.

The term web server usually refers to the software rather than the entire computer system (IIS, Apache or 3rd party). The web server manages requests from the browser and delivers the HTML documents and files to the client in answer to requests. Any server-side scripts written in CGI, JSPs, ASP, Perl, VBScript, or C will also be executed by the web server.

The two main web servers commonly used are IIS and Apache. Apache has derived from a Linux platform and is currently adopted by over 69% of the industry because of the benefits of its open source code. An Apache web server also offers benefits in speed of operation over an IIS server, however I personally have found it a little more complex to install and configure. A preferred option to about 24% of the industry is the use of an IIS server. This software is offered as part of the Windows package. The remaining 7% of web servers use third party applications, some of which are free on the internet and can be downloaded from shareware sites.

3.11 IIS (Internet Information Services)

Internet Information Services (IIS) published by Microsoft is part of Windows XP Professional. It allows you to publish your web pages quite easily on the internet or your intranet. A broad range of features are also available with IIS for managing websites and the server.

Active Server Pages (ASPs) allow the user to make more flexible websites that can accept input from the client to be processed by the web server, such as feedback or enquiry forms. IIS is not installed by default but can be added using the Add/Remove Programs dialog box from the Control Panel. For more information, see Installing IIS under the help facility in your windows installation or by visiting the Microsoft website.

IIS Professional can only service ten simultaneous client connections, which may be an issue for some organisations.

IIS Software Checklist

Before you install IIS, you need to install the Windows TCP/IP Protocol and Connectivity Utilities.

The following optional components are recommended:

- The Domain Name System (DNS) service installed on a computer in your intranet. If your intranet is small, you can use Hosts or Lmhosts files on all computers in your network. This step is optional, but it allows users to use friendly text names instead of IP addresses. On the internet, websites typically use DNS. If you register a domain name for your site, users can type your site's domain name in a browser to contact your site.

- All your drives should be formatted with NTFS. This will allow you to implement adequate security features such as user permissions and share permissions. This will restrict access to specific areas of the web server, hard drive or folders.

IIS Installation

There are many options during the installation process. These include Common Files, Documentation and the Internet Information Services snap-in. It is your choice whether you install any of these items. My advice is that if you have the hard drive space, do a full installation as you may need these items at a later date and it's a real bind going back and reinstalling options later on. Another point to remember is that disabling certain options can reduce the functionality of IIS. If you are not confident of carrying out the installation of IIS, then stick to the default settings. After you install IIS, you can view Installing IIS Optional Components in the IIS online documentation for more information.

To install IIS, add optional components, or remove optional components:

1) Click Start, click Control Panel, and click Add or Remove Programs.

2) Click Add/Remove Windows Components. The Windows Components Wizard appears.

3) Follow the on-screen instructions to install, remove, or add components to IIS.

Once you have IIS installed which shouldn't take you more than fifteen minutes, you can double click on the IIS icon and view the running web server. This is the location of where your site will be stored and then hosted. Sub directories or folders can be created and then your site placed in one of those allowing the webmaster to host several sites with URLs pointing to the individual index pages in their respective folders.

The need to install a Web Server

In the majority of cases for simple websites employing only html pages you can test their functionality simply by opening a browser and viewing the pages. For more complex websites that have ASP (Active Server Pages), a web server such as IIS is required for testing. Simply loading these ASP pages in your browser and by-passing the server will result in the page not loading.

In addition to ASPs, if you use any other scripts, then testing your website through the server will also be necessary.

Part 4
Your Website's Commercial Potential

4.1   Earning Money from your Website

My very good friend, who shall remain nameless, often phones me and asks if I can think of any ideas on how he can make money on the internet. The fact is, every website can earn money but it's dependant upon many factors including your personal vision, drive, marketing ability as well as having a good idea and a quality website.

One of my first websites I owned earned a grand total of zero. The reason for this was I didn't have anyone advising me on how to manage it effectively. My second web site earned more, and the beautiful thing about it is that I never had to leave home to do it.

There is a website on the internet for virtually every topic and idea you can think of. That doesn't mean you cannot construct a website for a similar or even the same topic and still make some money out of it. After all when you visit a city you will find more than one dealership selling cars. The difficult part is being more successful than your competitor.

Success on the internet these days has become competitive and challenging. I am confident that there are still ideas and projects out there to be developed that will earn millions for a lucky few, but it does require some innovative thinking. The favourite one I am usually presented with is the porn site. If I have come across one male student that comes up with this idea as his master plan for earning big bucks in the web business then I have met a thousand. The slightly troubling thought with this is that I am concerned they might be right and I am missing an opportunity. The question to be asked is, "Can there ever be too many porn sites out there?" There is no doubt that they certainly earn money. But my real quest in this book is to provide you with guidance on how to achieve the full potential with a website, not to provide you with ideas.

Some years ago, we all witnessed the boom in .com businesses. It was the in-thing to have one, and banks seemed eager to invest large sums of money in ventures on the internet. Everyone seemed to have the belief that failure was impossible. Millions were invested only to see most of them dwindle into obscurity. There are success stories though and with the right ideas and business sense, perhaps your website will be next!

4.2 The Million Dollar Pixel Story

During 2005, 21 year old Alex Tew came up with a crazy idea of selling pixels for $1 each to help fund his university attendance. The idea was born out of desperation and wasn't expected to be become as successful as it is today or be imitated by so many other companies. Basically Alex Tew wanted to sell one million pixels. His site consisting of nothing but advertisements provided a minimum of 100 pixels per advert (10 pixels by 10 pixels).

In August of 2005, one month before starting university the Million Dollar Pixel site was born. Within the first two weeks, Alex had earned $40,000. Within six months earnings were close on $600,000 and with unique hits of over 200,000 per week.

It's a simple idea, but it worked and earned big money. I wish I'd thought of that one! However, thinking of the right idea that works is the challenge. Alex's success was as much down to gaining excellent publicity. He appeared on television and radio which would have certainly increased the number of hits on his site. This confirms that an effective marketing campaign is crucial to your success on the web.

4.3 Google's Story

Google is now one of the most popular search engines in use on the internet. From its birth in 1995 to 2006 Google has seen substantial growth and dominance and is one of the most successful companies on the web. Google is a play on the word googol and refers to the number represented by the numeral one followed by 100 zeros. Google's use of the term reflects the company's mission to organise the immense information on the web. So, how did Google come about?

1995 – 1997
Google founders Larry Page and Sergey Brin met at the University of Standford in the computer science department. Larry was a 24 year old University of Michigan student on a weekend visit. Sergey was a 23 year old student that was assigned to show Larry around. During January of 1996 the two started to work together and were developing a search engine called BackRub named for its unique ability to analyse the 'back links' pointing to a given website. Larry was known for his hardware skills and had taken on the task of building servers from low end computers instead of large expensive machines.

1998
During the early part of 1998 the pair purchased a terabyte of disk storage and started to build their own servers in Larry's dorm room. Sergey set up business premises and they began calling on potential partners who might want to license a search technology better than any that was available. David Filo, friend and Yahoo founder, was one of those people they called upon. David agreed that their technology was solid and

encouraged the partnership to grow and form a search engine company.

Andy Bechtolsheim, a founder of Sun Microsystems, helped the partnership out. He recognised the potential Larry and Sergey had developed. His time was limited but they did secure a cheque from him for $100,000 made out to Google Inc which of course didn't exist at this time.

September 1998 Google Inc was started in Menlo Parik, California. The corporate office was attached to a garage of a friend. The first employee was Craig Silverstein who became Google's director of technology. At this point Google.com was answering 10,000 search enquiries each day. With the aid of press articles, reviews that appeared in USA TODAY and Le Monde, Google grew fast. In December 1998 PC Magazine named Google one of its Top 100 websites and search engines for 1998.

1999

By February 1999 Google moved on to an office on University Avenue in Palo Alto. Eight staff were now answering 500,000 search requests per day. During June of that year Google secured a further $25 million from SiliconValley companies Sequoia Capital and Kleiner Perkins Caufield & Byers. Mike Morits of Sequoia and John Doerr of Kleiner Perkins took seats on Google's board of directors.

Google was now hiring key people from other organisations, such as Kordestani from Netscape who accepted a position as Vice President of business development and sales. Urs Hölzle from UC Santa Barbara was hired as vice president of engineering. The overcrowded offices meant a further move to Googleplex, Google's current headquarters in Mountain View, California.

Recognition of Google now meant that AOL and Netscape selected Google as its web search engine and helped push traffic past the 3 million searches per day. On September 21, 1999, the beta label was removed off the website and with further expansion and growth the Italian portal Virgilio signed on as a client together with Virgin Net.

2001
Google became available in 26 languages. Further amendments were made to Google's search engine. In December, Google Image search was launched with 250 million images available within its index. The Google Catalogue Search was launched making it possible for Google users to search and browse more than 1,100 mail order catalogues. During December the search index reached 3 billion searchable web documents.

2002
Google's success as one of the internet's most widely used search engines was acknowledged in February at the Search Engine Watch Awards for Outstanding Search Service, Best Image Search Engine, Best Design, Most Webmaster Friendly Search Engine, and Best Search Feature.

February also saw Google's self-service advertising system 'Adwords' having a major overhaul. This included a cost-per-click CPC pricing model that made search advertising as cost effective for small businesses as large ones. Google's philosophy is and always has been to focus on the user.

In September, Google news was launched offering 4,500 leading news sources from around the world. Users could scan, search and browse headlines and photos. Foogle was launched in December and offered users an opportunity to search for multiple sources of specific products and then delivering images and prices for the items sought.

2003

Further innovations took place in Google world. They acquired Pyra Labs that became a home for Blogger, a leading provider of services for those inclined to share their thoughts through online journals.

Further releases included Version 2.0 of the Google Toolbar with Google Deskbar joining it in the autumn. The new version included a pop-up blocker and form filler. The Deskbar fitted in on the Windows Taskbar and made it possible to search using Google without even launching a web browser.

2004

Google was named as 'Brand of the Year' for 2003 by Brandchannel. The site index increased to 4.28 billion web pages. During February, Google announced an expanded web index of more than 6 billion items which included the 4.28 billion web pages plus 880 million images and 845 million Usenet messages.

On April 1st, Google announced its plans to open a research facility on the moon and a new web-based mail service called Gmail offering each user a gigbyte of storage. Gmail wasn't an April Fool's joke and proved to be a powerful function. On April 29, Google filed with the SEC for an initial public offering (IPO). An announcement was made during June of a new version of the Google Search Appliance with a capacity for more than 300 queries per minute and the ability to scale from 150,000 to 15 million or more documents.

Picasa based in Pasadena, California was a digital photo management company that was acquired by Google during

July. August marked the initial public offering of GOOGLE on NASDAQ through a little-known Dutch auction process, which is designed to attract a broader range of investors than the usual IPO often does.

During October Google announced quarterly revenues of $805.9 million, up 105% on the previous year. Google also acquired Keyhole Corp, a digital and satellite image mapping company based in Google's own headquarters town. This acquisition gave Google a powerful new search tool to view 3D images across the world.

The new European offices opened in Dublin with 150 employees from 35 different countries. Nikesh Arora joined Google in London as senior executive overseeing Google's operations in the European market. December marked the month for the launch of Google Groups, a new version of the Usenet archive of 1 billion posts of thousands of topics.

2005
Further growth aided by the acquisition of San Diego-based web analytics firm Urchin Software and popularity of blogs and feeds helped Google's development. Google Sitemaps was launched in June enabling webmasters to publish their pages on the web. Google Earth unveiled in late June enabled users to fly through space, zooming into specific locations, and seeing the real world in sharp focus. In July, Google opened a new Chinese R&D centre and hired Dr. Kai Fu-Lee. Google saw the release of Google Talk in August, a free way to actually speak to people anytime, anywhere via your computer, featuring crystal-clear voice technology. The next generation of Google Desktop was also released.

Google Base was launched in mid November offering users a new way to upload content – lists, web pages and items of any type in a structured format that interested searchers can find. This would include items for sale or scientific data or such simple things as recipes. The year closed with the addition of two new members to the board of directors: Dr. Shirley Tilghman and Ann Mather.

2006

A brand new store called Google Video was launched enabling users to download media and play it on a new Google Video Player.

Google's Future?

It's hard to imagine what is next for Google. Every year sees Google grow from strength to strength with new acquisitions and launches. What is certain from looking at the history of Google is that they will not be left behind in the world of the internet.

However amongst every success story there are many stories of failure, whether it is from bad website design or management. The story of Boo.com is one of those most noted.

Boo.com

Boo.com was amongst one of Britain's top fashion sites that played part of the 90s dot com boom and crash era. Covering 18 countries, the company sold sports and street wear on the internet but due to a number of critical management errors crashed in May 2000.

In my opinion errors were made in both the management of the website and in the design. The trouble with many .com companies in the 1990s was that failure was considered unlikely if not impossible and therefore money was poured in to them with the belief that millions would be made in profits. History now shows that this was not the case and that all .coms have to be managed like any other business.

Boo.com has managed to take top place in a compilation of 101 "Dumbest Moments in e-Business History" published by eCompany, a San Francisco-based magazine belonging to the Fortune group.

The Management

The original shopping site was rumoured to have spent $150,000 in annual salaries for the founders, a further $100,000 each to rent apartments in London and an additional $100,000 for redecorating. An additional $650,000 was spent on promotional giveaways. With a venture capital of $135million, you can see the money would soon disappear. The biggest expenditure rumoured to have taken place was an advertising campaign costing $42million. With a staff of 420 people, offices in New York, Paris, Munich and Stockholm and with fashion consultants and hairstylists at a cost of $5,000 a day. Is it surprising that the company ran into trouble having spent all this money in under a year?

The Website

The design of the website did not help either. Users were required to have the Flash plug-in installed in their browser and with the website containing animations all over the place, users had to navigate their way around them to find the pages they wanted. This broke many if not the majority of the heuristics for designing an interface.

Users reported that the website locked up frequently within the browser and that pop-up windows were launched almost constantly. Pop-ups are one aspect that users hate and if you have a pop-up blocker, this can inhibit the full operation of any website.

With too many graphics on the site and no text based alternative for users, the speed of download was slow. A fast internet connection was required for download due to all the graphics and animations present on all the pages. Mac users could not access the website at all.

If fact, I think even one of my first year National Certificate students could identify the majority of the web design faults made on the Boo.com website. The website had every feature possible to make users shy away from using the website, designed more for entertainment than for selling.

4.4 Ideas for Income Generation

So many people I meet are under the illusion that they can make money out of having a website without putting a great deal of effort into the task. A great number try and fail. Of course websites with an online store should earn money through the sale of products and services if marketed well. However I want to guide you through the process of how to earn potential income from general websites and not from selling a product or service. There are a great number of techniques you can implement that will generate income.

Several years ago I had an idea of writing a small search engine website. After a long uninspiring lesson on a Thursday afternoon with a group of my students, I decided to name my site www.crapsearch.com. A brief domain name search revealed that the name was still available much to my surprise. I hastily purchased the .com and .co.uk domain name and sat back confident I had stumbled across a little goldmine of an idea. Most of the code had already been written and I quickly created a simple search interface along the lines of Google.

I launched the site on a day that was as ordinary as the next, with no champagne or celebrity present. I sat back and monitored the traffic. A few strategically placed adverts and links through other sites based on a commission basis were all put in place. I watched the hits grow from 500 to 1,750 per day. This is not many compared to the giants of some search engines. However, I was earning around 5p from each hit on my site. I remember the first cheque I received, it was exciting and inspiring. I ran the website for a few months before selling to www.dogpile.com

Many search engines are bought-out by large ones that have better resources, technology and finances. Despite the increasing difficulties for search engines to survive solely on advertising, I think there will always be room for specialist small search engines fulfilling niche markets.

Income-Generating Advertising

To earn money from your website you'll need some strategically placed quality advertising. Better to focus on a few well placed adverts relevant to the content of the website instead of a large number of randomly placed abstract adverts.

Sites that contain purely adverts and banners are doomed to fail. However, I have to hold my hands up to Alex Tew for his million dollar pixel advertising site. There is always one wacky idea that works out.

Making a site interesting is the key then you need to populate it with a few well placed advertisements relating to the page content. You don't need a great number of visitors to earn money. Using commission based advertisements mean that every time somebody visits your site and then clicks on the advertisement and buys a product from the link, you will earn some money.

The two main types of advertisers you can get are banner adverts and affiliate programs, as previously mentioned. I favour the affiliate programs as banner adverts seem to be fading from popularity.

To reiterate, the popular banner ads are pay-per-click (CPC) and pay-per-view (CPM). Pay-per-click will pay you money every time someone clicks on the banner. Pay-per-view will pay you every time the banner is loaded into someone's browser. Obviously pay-per-view is going to earn you a lot more money but these are not generally available to small websites. Pay-per-click advertising does not pay as well but with careful targeting you could generate a good number of clicks.

A new development is pay-per-action (CPA) banners where the user must do something on the advertiser's site for you to earn the money. This is similar to affiliate programs and may involve the user signing up for a newsletter.

Affiliate programs allow you to earn a percentage through the sale of a product or service. Amazon.com offers an affiliate program in the form of a search box. Place the search box on your site and if your website visitor uses it and buys an item from Amazon then you earn a percentage of the sale.

These schemes usually have a minimum limit before payout. So you may have to reach £100 before receiving a cheque. You should read through the terms and conditions when signing up.

There is potential to earn large sums of revenue from the right affiliate schemes and this is certainly worth exploring.

Prize Incentives

On one website I owned, I used to get users to register by leaving their names and email addresses in order to win a prize. The value of the prize was carefully worked out so as not to exceed the potential revenue I could earn from the exercise. Each visitor that registered would generate £0.35. I sold on the details to ListBot who used the information for marketing. If I got 1000 users to register, I generated £350. The prize, a portable TV valued at £150, left me with a profit of £200 and having generated traffic to my website.

I would like to alert you to the legalities of selling mailing lists. You should seek legal advice of what disclosure you may need to make on your website informing your visitors of how their information may be used. If your visitors do subscribe to a list, you must provide adequate opportunities for them to opt-out or unsubscribe. Failure to do this could lead to legal action.

This type of income generation on a small scale isn't likely to make you a vast amount of money, however that doesn't mean you cannot earn a nice little amount of pocket money per month, say a couple of thousand pounds!

Advertising Revenue

The more people visiting your site the more successful you are going to become. As your site's traffic increases, other businesses and large organisations will want to advertise their products / services on your site giving you another income-generation opportunity! Imagine a website that has 10,000 visitors per day; wouldn't you want to advertise your services or products on that site?

Constant attention is always required to ensure that your website stays near the top of the search engine ratings and that the number of visitors to your website does not decrease. This task is all part of good website management and your marketing efforts.

4.5 Ecommerce Essentials

Online trading is the buying and selling of goods and services over electronic networks, whether between businesses or between businesses and consumers. Ecommerce describes how electronic networks are being harnessed to make efficiencies in the way information is processed within or between businesses.

Ecommerce is growing at a tremendous rate and faster than forecasts. Reports reveal a growth in the region of three million US internet users to one hundred million in under three years. Online trading in 2001 was valued as £6.5bn. Reports now show that trading in 2005 was around £300bn.

Ecommerce brings many changes to the way consumers live and do business and it has revolutionised shopping. There are many benefits from becoming involved in ecommerce. From experience within my own business I have found that I can automate processes and provide quick, efficient and effective support to my customers. Electronic links with other organisations can add value to the product or service I am selling. This in turn opens the way to customer growth through quality of support.

Ecommerce benefits:

- Access to new markets.
- Cost savings on marketing and promotion.
- Improved customer service.
- Longer lasting, more profitable customer relationships.
- Longer lasting, more profitable supplier relationships.

There are four basic items that must be in place for you to open a successful and secure online storefront:

- An Internet Merchant Account.
- Credit Card Transaction Processing.
- Shopping Cart Software.
- Secure Web Hosting.

Merchant Account

A merchant account allows you to accept credit card transactions. If you already have a bricks and mortar store, you probably already have a merchant account and chances are you can use that same one for your online store. If you don't have a physical store or aren't currently accepting credit cards, then one option is to apply for a merchant account with a bank.

Banks have different requirements for applying for merchant accounts; some require you to be in business for several years. Generally you must pay a set-up fee to get a merchant account. Then you'll also pay monthly fees and transaction fees based on a percentage of the credit card authorization. For more details about a merchant account contact your bank.

Credit Card Transaction Processing

Once a customer has given you their credit card number, you'll need some way of verifying the number and getting authorization for the credit card. Once you ship the item or deliver the service, you'll need to settle the transaction so the money can be deposited to your merchant account.

If you have an existing merchant account for a physical store, you can download your orders daily and process them using your existing procedures. If you don't already have a system in place for handling credit card transactions, then you'll need to find a company that can provide online realtime credit card authorizations for you. There are many companies specializing in this service, and sometimes credit card transaction processing is provided with an ecommerce shopping cart package.

Merchant Account Alternatives - WorldPay

WorldPay offers a secure method of payment for millions of people around the world who use the internet. The company is part of The Royal Bank of Scotland Group, the 5th biggest banking group in the world. Like other payment systems, Worldpay is used by individuals to large businesses. Payments can be accepted over the internet, by phone, fax or mail with all the major credit and debit cards being accepted. Bank transfers (such as the German ELV system), instalments, standing-order and direct-debit style payments are also accepted, all in the customer's currency and language - wherever they are in the world.

WorldPay was founded in 1993 with its European hardquarters established in Cambridge, UK in 1999. The company has been at the forefront of developing secure, comprehensive and straightforward e-payment processing systems ever since. In 1994 the first online shop offering secure transactions was opened followed by endorsement by Barclays

Bank in 1995. Multi-currency capability was developed in 1996/1997. During 2001 Worldpay established its Oklahoma call centre to support solutions in the US. It is now used by millions of people world wide for transactions on the internet.

Shopping Cart Software

Shopping carts provide an online catalogue for your customers to browse and an ordering feature for them to enter their personal information, including credit card details. There are many different shopping cart packages on the market. Some are hosted solutions, which include web hosting for the online store, and others installed on your own website. The packages vary greatly in the amount of customization to the look, feel and number of products you have in your store. Prices range from £100/month to £500/one-time purchase.

Secure Web Hosting

The importance of security for your online store cannot be understated. Although most online transactions are more secure than your average purchase from a bricks and mortar establishment, customers are skittish about providing their credit card information online. The right security can put them at ease. SSL (secure socket layer) is essential for providing security for your website. It ensures that credit card information is encrypted while it's being entered on your website. SSL is provided by your ISP or the company that hosts your website, and is generally not available as part of basic web hosting. You may need to upgrade to a different (and usually more expensive) web hosting package to use SSL.

Additionally, you can obtain a digital certificate that authenticates that you are who you say you are. Certificates are not required, but give customers added satisfaction of knowing that they are dealing with a reputable company.

4.6 The Future

I've been working in the computing industry now for over eighteen years and seen many changes and developments in technology and software. I've also been witness to projects that I thought were mad which have made millions and projects I thought brilliant fall flat on the ground.

So, what are my thoughts for the future? Well I would predict that with the development of the internet within China and the increase in access, the need for websites in Chinese will be a major development area during the next five years. China has one of the largest populations in the world at 1.3 billion people, and already the population are sampling the delights of information available through the internet. Censorship issues still exist, but I foresee these disappearing within the next couple of years. Out of the 1.3billion, only 33.7 million currently have internet access which amounts to 2.5%. Compare this to the UK where 55% have internet access.

There are many website designers on the market today, but how many of them can speak, read and write in Chinese, or mandarin?

If this is the case for China then India must also be in a similar position as they are the second largest population in the world. In India only 0.5% of the population is currently online. Maybe these countries are the new markets for the next shrewd web developer!

About ten years ago, internet access was more or less restricted to those that felt they could justify the cost of using the internet. As internet costs have dropped and high speed broadband access increased, greater uses for the internet have been brought in to the reach of everyone. Software has developed and become easier to use with better quality of interfaces available. This has enabled people with minimum computer skills to access the internet and use it as a tool for research or homework. PC banking, music downloads, shopping, and selling goods are all areas that have grown on the internet and so has the age range of people wanting to access those resources.

So with that in mind, my other prediction is that as time progresses and more of our daily routines become computerised and available through the internet the need for all of us to access and use the internet becomes a necessity. This includes the elderly. Over the past four years I have observed my own parents, who are in their seventies, become more reliant on the computer than ever before. What started off as a tool for browsing the internet and playing a few games has developed into a facility for checking their bank account, paying an electricity bill or ordering their shopping.

Have a look on the internet today and see how many websites you can find that target elderly people and provides them with resources and information that they may need. Perhaps you can come up with an idea for a new web venture!

Conclusion

I hope this book has provided you with a basic understanding of some of the principles that you can apply to your own website development and that it contributes towards your future success. I should stress that it can take years of experience and training to gain a full appreciation of the many factors that need to be implemented for effective and successful web design and management.

As you practise, you will gain experience along the way and you will quickly find out what works and what doesn't. You will also learn that glitches and technical issues are also part of the journey and will no doubt add to your stress levels! Once you've designed, launched and managed your site and, as a result, perhaps received some positive feedback or even some business from it, you will gain great satisfaction in knowing that you have created a successful website. Who knows, it could be the start of a successful new career!

Appendix

Glossary

ASP (Active Server Pages)

These are web pages that contain a script of some kind that is executed on the server side. The web server executes the script and delivers the web page back to the client's browser without any of the script code.

Apache

Open Source Code Web Server developed in 1995 by a group of approximately 20 volunteer programmers. The code is freely available for download and therefore can be adapted or tailored to individual needs. Apache is available for Unix and windows platforms.

CGI (Common Gateway Interface)

One of the original technologies developed for the internet. Not used so much now as it has been superseded by newer scripts and technology such as Perl and C.

CMS (Content Management System)

This is software that manages the content of a website through a database.

Fat 16 or Fat 32 (File Allocation Table)

This is a file structure used on Windows 95, 98, Millennium, 2000 and XP. It does not allow the user to implement any security features but is simpler to implement and administer for the novice user.

IIS (Internet Information Server)

Produced by Microsoft to run on its windows platform. IIS is web server software that is required to turn a computer into a web server.

Merchant Account

This is an account required by organisations wishing to accept credit cards or debit cards in return for selling goods or services. There are different types of merchant accounts available depending on whether the business is online, mail order or a shop.

Meta-Tags

These are general purpose tags you can put in the header portion of any document to specify some information about the page. These meta-tags can assist in search engine indexing.

MySQL

Is an open source code script that relies on SQL for processing the data in a database. MySQL can run on a Unix and windows system and is commonly used for web based applications.

NTFS (New Technology File System)

This is a file structure used on Windows XP, 2000 and older NT Operating Systems. It is an alternative file structure to FAT16 or FAT32 and offers added security and error correction features.

Phishing

An email scam sent to an unsuspecting user to fool them into visiting a website that looks like the genuine site and entering in financial information.

PHP (Hypertext Preprocessor)
Created in 1994 by Rasmus Lerdorf. In 1997 it was later redeveloped by Zeev Suraski and Andi Gutmans. This is an open source code server side script. Code is not viewable by the client as it is server based. Operates in a similar fashion to Perl or C. PHP can perform any task that can be done by CGI scripts but its strength is in how it works with various types of databases. PHP is also compatible across networks.

RSS (Real Simple Syndication)
This is a script or code that a web designer can include on their website to include a video or news feed or other similar feed to attract visitors.

Scumware
Software that hides within the browser and places links on websites that you visit to redirect you to other sites usually pornography or advertising sites.

SEM (Search Engine Marketing)
As well as using SEO techniques, SEM more frequently refers to marketing of a website to search engines through paid placements and adverts.

SEO (Search Engine Optimisation)
SEO is about optimising your web content to make the web pages attractive and visible so that they are picked by the search engines.

SERP (Search Engine Results Page)
Are listings or results, displayed for a particular search.

Spoof Email

This is an email that appears to be from the source person, but isn't. Most email programs like Outlook allow users to create an email name in the header information and then send it to the recipient. The address may be genuine or not but most definitely not from the person you think it may be from. Outgoing email servers rarely authenticate the source email address.

SSI (Server Side Includes)

This is a special function which allows you to tell the server to include something on your page. It could be some text or some CGI generated code.

SSL (Secure Socket Layer)

Is a protocol developed by Netscape that encrypts the data for transmission over the internet. SSL creates a secure connection between the client and the web server. The protocol has been approved by the IETF (Internet Engineering Task Force) as a standard protocol.

Web Server

Is a computer with an IP address and a domain name that delivers web pages to a client. To turn a computer in to a web server requires the installation of web server software such as Apache or IIS.

Domain Name Extensions

.ac – Ascension Island

.ad – Andorra

.ae – United Arab Emirates

.af – Afghanistan

.ag – Antigua and Barbuda

.ai – Anguilla

.al – Albania

.am – Armenia

.an – Netherlands Antilles

.ao – Angola

.aq – Antarctica

.ar – Argentina

.as – American Samoa

.at – Austria

.au – Australia

.aw – Aruba

.az – Azerbaijan

.ax – Aland Islands

.ba – Bosnia and Herzegovina

.bb – Barbados

.bd – Bangladesh

.be – Belgium

.bf – Burkina Faso

.bg – Bulgaria

.bh – Bahrain

.bi – Burundi

.bj – Benin

.bm – Bermuda

.bn – Brunei Darussalam

.bo – Bolivia

.br – Brazil

.bs – Bahamas

.bt – Bhutan

.bv – Bouvet Island

.bw – Botswana

.by – Belarus

.bz – Belize

.ca – Canada

.cc – Cocos (Keeling) Islands

.cd – Congo, The Democratic Republic of the

.cf – Central African Republic

.cg – Congo, Republic of

.ch – Switzerland

.ci – Cote d'Ivoire

.ck – Cook Islands

.cl – Chile

.cm – Cameroon

.cn – China

.co – Colombia

.cr – Costa Rica

.cs – Serbia and Montenegro

.cu – Cuba

.cv – Cape Verde

.cx – Christmas Island

.cy – Cyprus

.cz – Czech Republic

.de – Germany

.dj – Djibouti

.dk – Denmark

.dm – Dominica

.do – Dominican Republic

.dz – Algeria
.ec – Ecuador
.ee – Estonia
.eg – Egypt
.eh – Western Sahara
.er – Eritrea
.es – Spain
.et – Ethiopia
.eu – European Union
.fi – Finland
.fj – Fiji
.fk – Falkland Islands (Malvinas)
.fm – Micronesia, Federal State of
.fo – Faroe Islands
.fr – France
.ga – Gabon
.gb – United Kingdom
.gd – Grenada
.ge – Georgia
.gf – French Guiana
.gg – Guernsey
.gh – Ghana
.gi – Gibraltar
.gl – Greenland
.gm – Gambia
.gn – Guinea
.gp – Guadeloupe
.gq – Equatorial Guinea
.gr – Greece
.gs – South Georgia and the South Sandwich Islands
.gt – Guatemala
.gu – Guam
.gw – Guinea-Bissau
.gy – Guyana
.hk – Hong Kong
.hm – Heard and McDonald Islands
.hn – Honduras
.hr – Croatia/Hrvatska
.ht – Haiti
.hu – Hungary
.id – Indonesia
.ie – Ireland
.il – Israel
.im – Isle of Man
.in – India
.io – British Indian Ocean Territory
.iq – Iraq
.ir – Iran, Islamic Republic of
.is – Iceland
.it – Italy
.je – Jersey
.jm – Jamaica
.jo – Jordan
.jp – Japan
.ke – Kenya
.kg – Kyrgyzstan
.kh – Cambodia
.ki – Kiribati
.km – Comoros
.kn – Saint Kitts and Nevis
.kp – Korea, Democratic People's Republic
.kr – Korea, Republic of
.kw – Kuwait
.ky – Cayman Islands

.kz – Kazakhstan
.la – Lao People's Democratic Republic
.lb – Lebanon
.lc – Saint Lucia
.li – Liechtenstein
.lk – Sri Lanka
.lr – Liberia
.ls – Lesotho
.lt – Lithuania
.lu – Luxembourg
.lv – Latvia
.ly – Libyan Arab Jamahiriya
.ma – Morocco
.mc – Monaco
.md – Moldova, Republic of
.mg – Madagascar
.mh – Marshall Islands
.mk – Macedonia, The Former Yugoslav Republic of
.ml – Mali
.mm – Myanmar
.mn – Mongolia
.mo – Macau
.mp – Northern Mariana Islands
.mq – Martinique
.mr – Mauritania
.ms – Montserrat
.mt – Malta
.mu – Mauritius
.mv – Maldives
.mw – Malawi
.mx – Mexico

.my – Malaysia
.mz – Mozambique
.na – Namibia
.nc – New Caledonia
.ne – Niger
.nf – Norfolk Island
.ng – Nigeria
.ni – Nicaragua
.nl – Netherlands
.no – Norway
.np – Nepal
.nr – Nauru
.nu – Niue
.nz – New Zealand
.om – Oman
.pa – Panama
.pe – Peru
.pf – French Polynesia
.pg – Papua New Guinea
.ph – Philippines
.pk – Pakistan
.pl – Poland
.pm – Saint Pierre and Miquelon
.pn – Pitcairn Island
.pr – Puerto Rico
.ps – Palestinian Territories
.pt – Portugal
.pw – Palau
.py – Paraguay
.qa – Qatar
.re – Reunion Island
.ro – Romania
.ru – Russian Federation
.rw – Rwanda

.sa – Saudi Arabia
.sb – Solomon Islands
.sc – Seychelles
.sd – Sudan
.se – Sweden
.sg – Singapore
.sh – Saint Helena
.si – Slovenia
.sj – Svalbard and Jan Mayen Islands
.sk – Slovak Republic
.sl – Sierra Leone
.sm – San Marino
.sn – Senegal
.so – Somalia
.sr – Suriname
.st – Sao Tome and Principe
.sv – El Salvador
.sy – Syrian Arab Republic
.sz – Swaziland
.tc – Turks and Caicos Islands
.td – Chad
.tf – French Southern Territories
.tg – Togo
.th – Thailand
.tj – Tajikistan
.tk – Tokelau
.tl – Timor-Leste
.tm – Turkmenistan
.tn – Tunisia
.to – Tonga
.tp – East Timor

.tr – Turkey
.tt – Trinidad and Tobago
.tv – Tuvalu
.tw – Taiwan
.tz – Tanzania
.ua – Ukraine
.ug – Uganda
.uk – United Kingdom
.um – United States Minor Outlying Islands
.us – United States
.uy – Uruguay
.uz – Uzbekistan
.va – Holy See (Vatican City State)
.vc – Saint Vincent and the Grenadines
.ve – Venezuela
.vg – Virgin Islands, British
.vi – Virgin Islands, U.S.
.vn – Vietnam
.vu – Vanuatu
.wf – Wallis and Futuna Islands
.ws – Western Samoa
.ye – Yemen
.yt – Mayotte
.yu – Yugoslavia
.za – South Africa
.zm – Zambia
.zw – Zimbabwe

Printed in the United Kingdom
by Lightning Source UK Ltd.
136330UK00001B/172-261/A